SCREENWRITING

"As a screenwriting educator I am frequently asked the twin questions: (1) Can writing be taught at all? (2) Can the formal study of writing really help a writer join the professional film and television community?

The second answer first: yes.

As this book's section of Script Sales Strategies attests, there is one best strategy—the only strategy—for a writer hoping to enter the film and television industry: good writing. To that end anything helping a writer structure his story, focus his characters, render his dialogue more palpable, more provocative, and any clue which in even a small way confronts the writer's relentless challenge to create a screenplay worthy of an audience, ought to go some fair distance toward bridging the chasm between amateur and professional.

But can writers truly be taught to write well? Simply stated, yes."

—Richard Walter, in his Introduction

RICHARD WALTER is Professor and Screenwriting Faculty Chairman in the Department of Theater Arts: Division of Motion Pictures & Television at UCLA. He has written numerous screenplays, including *American Graffiti*, and several movie novelizations.

D0451343

Screenwriting

The Art, Craft and Business
of Film and Television Writing

Richard Walter

A PLUME BOOK

NEW AMERICAN LIBRARY

NEW YORK AND SCARBOROUGH, ONTARIO

For Harry Warshawsky,
bookbinder, night worker

NAL BOOKS ARE AVAILABLE AT QUANTITY DISCOUNTS WHEN
USED TO PROMOTE PRODUCTS OR SERVICES. FOR INFOR-
MATION PLEASE WRITE TO PREMIUM MARKETING DIVISION,
NEW AMERICAN LIBRARY, 1633 BROADWAY, NEW YORK,
NEW YORK 10019.

PLUME TRADEMARK REG. U.S. PAT. OFF. AND FOREIGN COUNTRIES
REGISTERED TRADEMARK—MARCA REGISTRADA
HECHO EN CHICAGO, U.S.A.

SIGNET, SIGNET CLASSIC, MENTOR, ONYX, PLUME, MERIDIAN
and NAL BOOKS are published *in the United States* by
NAL PENGUIN INC., 1633 Broadway, New York, New York 10019,
in Canada by The New American Library of Canada Limited,
81 Mack Avenue, Scarborough, Ontario M1L 1M8

Library of Congress Cataloging-in-Publication Data

Walter, Richard, 1944–
  Screenwriting : the art, craft, and business of film and
television writing / Richard Walter.
      p.   cm.
  ISBN 0-452-26086-8 (pbk.)
  1. Motion picture authorship.   2. Television authorship.
3. Motion picture plays—Technique.   4. Television plays—Technique.
I. Title.
PN1996.W25   1988
808′.066791—dc19   88-1813
                                                                      CIP

First Printing, August, 1988

1   2   3   4   5   6   7   8   9

PRINTED IN THE UNITED STATES OF AMERICA

Acknowledgments

Virtue, Aristotle advises, is a necessary but insufficient element of the fulfilled life. A person needs also to be lucky.

My own luck is good in the extreme. First, throughout the decades I have been inspired and chastised by the world's best teachers. Four among many who opened my eyes and rapped my knuckles are: Yetta Rosenblum, who taught me to write with light; Nat Werner, who asserted that it is important for artists to be unimportant; Charlie Dennis, who cautioned me never to short-chop my stroke; and Irwin R. Blacker, who instilled in me the preference for a good movie over an important film.

And I am blessed also with the world's best students. They are for the most part in and of UCLA's Division of Film and Television. They challenge me to challenge myself and to beware of too much comfort. They are a fountain of talent in a bastion of discipline, fellow warriors in art's central struggle: the battle against boredom. May their glow brighten screens across the universe.

Thanks, also, to my Westwood colleagues, notably John W. Young who flees no fight; Donald Crabs, a man of faith; Robert H. Gray who cares passionately for art and artists; and George L. Schaefer, forever the new kid on our block.

And a breathless, hurting hug for the world's softest heart and most generous hand, guiding light of the UCLA

Writers' Bloc, the best and biggest buddy belonging to writers across the globe, my good friend: Lewis Ray Hunter.

And to Bill Froug, mahalo moemoea. Ho ohana a hano hano. Me kealoha.

And special things to Geoffrey Grode, the world's best guest lecturer.

And long-overdue appreciation to Arthur Knight for decades of limitless attention, consideration, encouragement, and support.

And gratitude also to my tireless and resourceful research assistant, Victoria Moore.

Thanks also to my faithful and affectionate grenades-on-his-belt commando at Curtis Brown Ltd., Henry Dunow.

And to NAL's Arnold Dolin, a wise and patient soul who, like all good editors and teachers, knows how to be both gentle and strict; and also to Gary Luke, who now appreciates halvah, for helping to keep me honest.

And to Andy Bergman for permitting me to reproduce a page of our 1973 screenplay, *Jackie Whitefish*.

And for David and Esther, about whom much more shall be said in future volumes.

And finally, most of all, with love, for Pat, Susanna, and Daniel, for tolerating the late nights, and for refusing to tolerate the weekends.

Special Appreciation

Special appreciation is due the UCLA Faculty Senate Committee on Research for its support—spiritual and financial—in this book's earliest stages and throughout its writing.

Contents

On the Use of Personal Pronouns

In the interest of clarity and economy, the personal pronouns "he," "him," and "his" as used in this book often may be taken also to mean "he or she," "him or her," and "his or her(s)."

INTRODUCTION:

The God Game

In the early seventies, while I was still nominally a student at USC's film school but had been writing professionally for a couple of years, the Writers Guild went on strike.

May I confess here and now that I loved the strike?

By that time I'd written half a dozen studio feature screenplays and had earned something resembling a steady and even a substantial living. But at that precise moment I was "between assignments"—Hollywood's euphemism for out of work—and I was not, therefore, rudely and summarily forced to abandon any post. The bright side of unemployment is that you cannot be fired.

It was springtime in Los Angeles and, notwithstanding my still-fresh New York chauvinism, I could not deny the season's sweetness. I lived in a comfy, cozy house with a big bright yard and fruit trees, birds, possums, skunks. I even liked the skunks. Inside my head I noodled around with a notion for a novel, but mainly, from my paneled north-light study, I stared serenely at the snowcapped San Gabriels.

At that particular moment a strike bothered me not a bit; indeed, I viewed the prospect as really rather appealing. And the best part by far was picket duty.

Twice a week, Guild members were required to present

themselves at a particular studio—my assignment was Paramount—and walk the line for all of three hours. Frankly, it was a joy. It got me out-of-doors and into the sunshine, caused me ever so slightly to utilize my muscles. But best of all, it was the first time ever in my life that I enjoyed the opportunity regularly to meet with other writers.

Parading with my colleagues up and back before the studio's Bronson gate, being writers, endlessly we talked. We talked sex. We talked sports. We talked weather. We talked cars. We talked Watergate.

But mainly we talked writing; not the profound, penetrating questions regarding beauty and truth but the hard-bitten, nuts/bolts considerations, working writers' shoptalk: hand-cranked versus electric pencil sharpeners, standard-versus legal-sized ruled yellow pads, felt-tipped markers versus ballpoint pens, liquid White Out versus cut-rate bulk generic correction fluid available by the half-gallon at one office supply outlet on Lake just north of Colorado in Pasadena.

Spoiled brats as we were, as all writers are and have been since the invention of writing in ancient Sumeria five thousand years ago, we catalogued all the horrific injustices we had suffered at the hands of executives, agents, collaborators: the lightweight pal-of-the-producer hack who had rewritten and wrecked our latest draft; the director who had butchered our most recent triumph; the agent who had refused to take or return our call; the civilian—spouse, child, parent, pal, pet, plant—who in some random gesture had neglected to pay ample homage to our boundless, fathomless genius.

Walking that line, talking with my fellows, midst all the show biz gossip, there emerged for me one startling, liberating discovery: *All writers hate to write!* I learned it was not I alone who dreaded the blank page, who struggled daily to drag himself to the desk, who dawdled and procrastinated and picked lint from the carpet in order to avoid actually applying fingers to keys. No, indeed, those nasty habits belong, I discovered, to all writers.

This may appear broodingly cynical, but it is simply a statement of observed fact. To sit all alone in a room, hour after hour, attempting to fill blank paper—or, these days, luminescent green phosphor—with story, character, and dialogue worth the time and attention of an audience is about as lonely as it gets. To be sure, writers love having written. But every last one of us hates to write. Writing, like banging your head against the wall, feels terrific mainly when you stop.

On our picket rounds, putting one foot in front of the other along Melrose, turning the corner at Van Ness, we inventoried the clever and elaborate methods by which the lot of us evade our task. One writer described a technique he had developed whereby he gazed blankly from his window at traffic; as soon as the fourteenth car bearing Nebraska plates drove past, he promptly started writing. Another claimed he would put quiet jazz on the stereo in the background, sharpen all his pencils, lay out neat, fresh stacks of heavy-gauge rag-content bond, and then, at long last . . . defrost the refrigerator.

This is not to deny that there are soaring, triumphant moments attendant to writing. Professional screenwriters are paid, after all, for the very same activity that gets other people scolded: daydreaming. Indeed, William Faulkner is said to have divorced his first wife because she could not understand that when he appeared to be staring idly out the window he was actually hard at work.

More than merely dreaming, in the course of scattered manic flashes writers do nothing less than play God. As God created the universe, each writer creates the universe of his screenplay. If he wants it to rain, it rains. If he wearies of rain and covets sunshine, out comes the sun. If he gets mad at somebody and wants to kill him—and who has never wanted to kill somebody?—a screenwriter kills him. And afterward, should he feel remorse, he can bring him back to life.

After too many years of auteurism, that alien notion anointing the director as film's first artist, screenwriters are at long last coming into their own, winning the recognition properly due movies' authentic prime movers. The writer truly is film's first artist if for no other reason than that he is truly first. The vast, sprawling army of film craftspeople are lost, every one of them, until a writer creates a plan. And that plan, of course, is the screenplay. The fanciest state-of-the-art cameras, the newest high-tech editing equipment, the best actors, the whole host of paraphernalia required for the production of a film is useless until a writer writes his plan.

The story is told of director Frank Capra, who was asked in an interview to explain precisely how he achieved that special quality known as "the Capra touch." For page after page he rambled on about this technique and that one. At great length he discussed how he had lent "the touch" to this film and to that one. And in all of these pages nowhere was mentioned Robert Riskin, who had merely written the films.

The day after the interview appeared in the press, there arrived at Capra's office a script-sized envelope. Inside was a document very closely resembling a screenplay: a front cover, a back cover, and one hundred and ten pages. But the cover and pages were all blank.

Clipped to the "script" was a note to Capra from Robert Riskin. It read: "Dear Frank, put the 'Capra touch' on *this*!"

Writing, like all creative expression, for all its struggle represents in the end a kind of structured, organized, orchestrated dreaming. That's why the writer's most basic task—before tale, before character and dialogue—is to learn how to let himself dream in a free yet orderly fashion.

But can people really be taught how to dream?

As a screenwriting educator I am frequently asked the twin questions: Can writing be taught at all? Can the formal study of writing really help a writer join the professional film and television community?

The second answer first. Yes.

As Chapter 9, "Script Sales Strategies," asserts, there is

one best strategy—the only strategy—for a writer hoping to enter the film and television industry: good writing. To that end anything helping a writer structure his story, focus his characters, render his dialogue more palpable, more provocative, any clue that in even a small way confronts the writer's relentless challenge to create a screenplay worthy of an audience, ought to go some fair distance toward bridging the chasm between amateur and professional.

But can writers truly be taught to write well?

Simply stated, yes.

For writing, like all creative expression, depends not upon talent alone but also upon discipline. Each quality is rare, but the two in tandem are exponentially rarer still. The sorry truth is that a lot of talent and very little discipline will not carry an artist nearly so far as the converse combination. Naturally, no teacher or book can provide talent; writers must supply their own. And neither can any writer have inspiration unwillingly thrust upon him; he has to discover motivation within himself.

Happily, however, if teachers cannot provide talent, neither can they take talent away. And if no book can supply a neat, easy, freeze-dried formula for creating the perfect screenplay, there are tasks both broad and narrow that can be usefully addressed. The present volume's struggle is to help writers in their battle to integrate inspiration and discipline, for without one, the other, no matter how copiously supplied, is simply squandered.

As asserted repeatedly throughout this book, screenwriting is in its nature a schizophrenic enterprise. Writers are required not only to shatter themselves temporarily into a widely varying cast of characters, each possessing unique traits, but simultaneously they need also to accomplish assorted tasks that endlessly contradict one another.

They need to write for audiences at the same time as they write for themselves. They must deal with seemingly separate items—story, character, dialogue, and so many others—that are in fact not separate at all but exist only in combination with one another. Writers' minds must freely wander among an apparently infinite array of chaotic, scattered details even as they have to assert a clear, logical, inevitable order throughout the length and breadth of their scripts. They must write films that are wholly fantastic even as they are quite perfectly plausible. And like all artists, they must consistently tell nothing but the truth even though in order to do so requires perpetually that they lie through their teeth.

An Overview of the Present Volume

As underscored in Chapter 3, "Story: Tale Assembly," there is a vast difference between assembling a child's tricycle from the shipping crate on one hand and constructing an integrated screen story on the other. Most notably, the latter requires a considerable measure of magic.

This book is intended, therefore, to be much more than how-to-write-the-trillion-dollar-screenplay-in-three-easy-lessons. For there is so much more to screenwriting than knowing precisely how far to indent the dialogue. Readers possessed of a need to grasp proper screenplay format can turn immediately to Chapter 7, which treats this subject in considerable detail and contains also, at its conclusion, an example of a properly laid-out page from an actual screenplay.

Technique and format aside, an artist's unique spirit remains very much the central focus of his art. If writing for the screen is in so many ways a hands-on enterprise, writers need also consider the fundamental human, esthetic, and philosophical issues that for thousands of years have caused audiences to flock to theaters in search of spiritual and emotional nourishment.

Consider this book's structure to be something of an inverted pyramid. Starting at the bottom are a handful of precepts constituting the substance of Part I, General Considerations. This is the hardest, most commonly neglected aspect of writing; all the rest—craft, format, business—is relatively easy. But none of the latter can be purposefully addressed if the foundation is not first properly laid.

Part II, Nuts and Bolts, examines writing's more practical, day-to-day considerations, specific details relating to story, character, and dialogue among a host of other seemingly isolated yet actually interdependent components.

Part III, The Writing Habit, deals with writers' attitudes regarding their daily struggle to structure their dreams into screenplays meriting the time, attention, and consideration of audiences.

And since the movie not produced, the film not viewed by audiences, has precisely the same effect as the movie not written at all, Part IV, The Business—Script Sales Strategies, addresses the complex issues pertinent to integrating screenplays into the professional film and television community—agents, producers, actors, directors, lawyers, the whole catalogue of craftsmen and collaborators.

Far too often these latter items preoccupy the attention of inexperienced writers. As emphasized in this section, for writers to begin writing from the standpoint of marketing is a self-defeating prophesy. There is simply no need to worry about marketing material that has yet to be written. There is no useful purpose in writers concerning themselves about sales before they have something to sell. Contrary to popular misconception, finding an agent is easy; what is hard is writing a screenplay worthy of a responsible agent's representation.

Finally, having necessarily fractured screenwriting's aspects into hundreds of pieces, there is a conclusion, The Whole Picture, which attempts to put them all back together again. In the end, screenwriting, for all its loneliness, and notwithstanding its inevitable agonies, is seen, unarguably, also to be a most delicious addiction.

Chaim Potok, in his timeless novel *The Chosen*, describes a rabbi in conversation with his son. The Hebrew word for God, the rabbi explains, is *mel,* which means also "king" and "head."

The reverse of *mel,* the rabbi continues, *lem,* means precisely the opposite. It means "fool" and also "heart."

And therefore, the rabbi advises the boy, if he wants to live as a king, if he wants to emulate God, he must be ruled not by his heart but by his head.

Good advice for a rabbi's son, but not particularly so for writers. Writing is far more a heart-oriented enterprise, a creation of hands, of groin, than of intellect.

Writing for the screen is top to bottom a wondrously silly activity, a sweetly ridiculous way for grown men and women to ply their trade and live their lives.

If you want to be God or a king, therefore, let your head guide you. But should you wish to write for the screen, live by your heart: Seize the courage to be just a little bit of a fool.

PART I
GENERAL CONSIDERATIONS

IMPOLITE LANGUAGE:

Seven Naughty Words

As Screenwriting Faculty Chairman at UCLA's Division of Film and Television, I possess the authority to compel legions of students to purchase screenwriting books. Not surprisingly, publishers send me every title touching even remotely on the subject. These seem to flow nowadays at the rate of perhaps two a week. Among all these books some are fine, some are not. Some are desperately serious and self-important, some are lighthearted and breezy. But there is a single component uniting virtually all of them: a glossary.

Almost inevitably the glossary is replete with precisely the kind of technical film jargon I urge screenwriters at all costs to avoid: angles, lenses, camera moves, editing effects, fancy film graphics.

Screenplays should contain nothing besides clear, everyday language. It doesn't hurt a bit, of course, for a writer to be a genius of invention and imagination. But what he needs to know first of all is English. And he needs to know it quite well, since language is the sole tool available for transporting a screen story from the writer's own head into the heads of others.

Of particular importance is precision in the choice of words.

To that end, I present a glossary of precisely seven commonly misconstrued terms. Granted, in our modern age these words have taken on new meanings, but here I wish to argue for restoration of their original denotations, as current connotations engender snobbism, a danger to any art, and especially destructive to public and popular arts such as film and television.

And a note of caution is in order: In some circles the words that follow are considered no less than obscene; reader discretion is advised. But remember also that polite language, as Samuel Goldwyn said years ago, makes for polite pictures. And polite pictures violate movies' one inviolable rule: They're boring.

1. Entertainment

Year after year, upon the release of the latest James Bond installment, producer Albert Broccoli offers newspaper interviews reassuring the critics that he fully appreciates his 007 films represent "not *Macbeth*, just entertainment."

Does he not know how entertaining *Macbeth* is? That it has witches and riddles and special effects ("Is this a dagger I see before me?") and murder, mayhem, lust, greed, intrigue, sword fights, blood, vengeance, horror?

But surely there is more to *Macbeth*, scholars and critics remonstrate, than these mere surface tensions. And they are not wrong. For indeed, beneath the play's veneer lie profound insights into the most fundamental aspects of human nature.

Entertainment and poetry are not, however, mutually exclusive. To the contrary, they walk together in lockstep. And no artist—notably no film or television writer—need apologize for entertaining an assembled mass of people.

Over many years *entertainment* has acquired an unwarranted pejorative connotation; it has come to signify that which is fleeting, superficial, insubstantial. But truly to comprehend the term, a writer could do a lot worse than to check out a worthy dictionary.

And there is none worthier than the *Oxford English Dictionary.*

Therein *entertainment* is revealed to enjoy an honorable, venerable tradition. To entertain is to occupy, to hold, to give over to consideration as in "to entertain a notion." This suggests not painting one's face and performing a tap dance for the notion, but cradling it in one's cortex, hefting its spiritual mass, regarding it, weighing it, investing it with contemplation.

Entertain actually derives from *intertwine.* And entertainment is intertwinement in two special ways.

First is the weaving of all the elements—plot, character, dialogue, action, setting, and all the rest—into a unified body within a single work. And second is a film's union with its viewers, for, ideally, the viewer of any true art in a certain sense becomes part of the creation.

To entertain, it is unfairly asserted, is solely to divert. A film most certainly should achieve more than merely that, but it cannot accomplish anything at all unless first of all it entertains.

2. Commercialism

Commercialism derives, of course, from *commerce.* And decent, sensitive, genuinely inspired artists no sooner engage in commerce than in pedophilia. Commerce is, after all, mere trade. And it is not for nothing that respectable homes and hostelries have separate entrances—in the alley, around back, below stairs—for tradesmen.

Ought not the serious, self-respecting writer be free of the constraints tied to trafficking? How else is he to find—and ultimately to share with viewers—the profound truths lying at his core? How do we reconcile worthy art with sucking for bucks?

Once again, turn to the dictionary.

Commerce, notwithstanding its popular connotations, means also a great deal more than simply dealing. Like *entertainment,* the word possesses a respectable history. *Commerce* means first of all "to communicate physically," which all by itself is no shabby description of movies. More significantly, *commerce* suggests "intercourse or converse with God, with spirits, passions, thoughts." *Commerce* denotes "association, communication," especially with regard to "the affairs of life." It represents an "exchange between men of the products of nature or art."

One could travel light-years in search of a loftier, nobler definition of artistic integrity. To be sure, a film's commercial success alone does not establish its merit. But conversely, neither does broad commercial success automatically constitute worthlessness. And neither does remoteness and obscurity guarantee a film's vast value.

"A poet," said Orson Welles, "needs a pen, a painter a brush, and a filmmaker an army." Armies cost money. Commerce in movies and TV is no more than that vital mechanism necessary to communicate expression whose production happens to be costly.

So commerce's lowly reputation is undeserved. If a writer is too fancy to slug it out in the down-and-dirty world of commerce, that's his prerogative, but I urgently advise him to avoid slumming in film and television.

3. Voyeurism

Critics relentlessly assail certain films as voyeuristic, but precisely what are movies if not that? The viewers hide in the theater's darkness peering through the window of the screen into the personal and private lives of strangers. They paw their effects, scrutinize their moves, eavesdrop on their conversations.

Because we know better than to prowl real alleys peeping into real houses, we hire filmmakers to peep for us. If a film appears brazenly, heavy-handedly voyeuristic, it probably fails to exercise sufficient craft. But castigating film as voyeurism is like reprimanding water for wetness.

4. Contrivance

Film is the single most contrived enterprise in the history of the universe.

What is more disjointed, manipulated, and arranged than film? As audiences, we view scenes containing intercut shots, seemingly synchronous dialogue, even as in some remote recess of our consciousness we appreciate that the different pieces were recorded in many places and at widely varying times.

Contrivance, like all craft, should never show. A skillful screenplay appears, quite falsely, to be seamless. This notion is discussed in various chapters of this book; it is sufficient here simply to say that if you can't live with grandly crafted appearances, if you disdain fantasy and artifice, you ought not pursue screenwriting, for it is above all the art of maximum contrivance.

5. Exploitation

As a screenwriter you are in the wrong place, also, if you are too highly bred ever to engage in anything so low-class as exploitation.

In fact all art—not film alone—exploits in one way or another. *To exploit* means simply to make the most of, to extract the finest, richest resources, to achieve the highest expression. Good scripts are hard enough to construct without pulling punches, for screenwriting is basically a bare-knuckles enterprise. Writers seeking maximum effect need not fear to exploit their resources.

6. Hollywood

Hollywood—which is to say the professional film and television community in metropolitan Los Angeles—remains more than ever the center of First World filmmaking.

Is it the sunshine? Southern California has no monopoly on sunshine. Is it tradition? Film is still far too young a medium to have much in the way of tradition. Is it the abundance of skilled craftsmen?

Possibly.

But even if most Hollywood films fail, if so many of them are shallow and superficial, so also are most books, poems, songs, paintings. The nature of artistic experimentation is explored in a later chapter. But if you turn up your nose at mention of the word *Hollywood,* if you can't tolerate tinsel, if you don't like bright, brash, brassy attention-craving spectacle, crisp, crazy dialogue, broad, sprawling action and fleshy, flashy effects, probably somewhere you took a wrong turn in your development as a practitioner of public, popular art.

7. Audience

In film and in television, *audience* is quite possibly the most important word of all. And in elitist circles it is also the naughtiest.

In a book on screenwriting, audience ought to represent a principle so essential as to merit primary position in a chapter treating the art's foremost fundamental issues. And in any such self-respecting book that chapter ought to follow immediately.

ESSENTIAL PRINCIPLES

Audience: The Status of the Observer

Movies are for audiences.

Should a painting, for example, find even a single patron it may survive throughout the ages. Should a poem receive even the narrowest publication, it may eventually come to be celebrated by masses of readers into eternity. But this is simply not true for film.

The public and popular arts are for the public and populace. Truly to fulfill their natural purpose, movies require a collected group, not an observer but a broad multiplicity of observers, all of them viewing the work together in relatively large congregations, the lot of them watching the work unfold at a steady, single pace.

Preoccupation with observers is nothing new to the current era; indeed, the focus of twentieth-century intellect in art as well as science is precisely that.

Einstein's theory of relativity is an example. While it led eventually to nuclear energy, its ultimate effect was simply to elevate the status of the observer. Questions, after Einstein, came to require not answers but only further questions. What is truth? The answer lies in the twin questions: For whom? From where? Truth has come to be viewed as irrevocably integrated into the particular vantage belonging to the observer.

The observer of a movie is its audience. A movie without an audience has the same effect as a movie that does not exist. To be sure, it may exist in some technical way—clumps of silver halide crystals clouding a chemical emulsion, patterns of light and shadow married to a celluloid base. But without viewers, a film has the same effect as if it simply had not been created in the first place. It touches nobody. It moves no one. Without an audience to observe it, all the talent and toil embedded within it add up to zero. No screenwriter, therefore, may ignore audience.

Consider a remote radio station of limited broadcast range. Imagine a lone disc jockey with a late-night jazz show. The jockey realizes his program enjoys but a handful of listeners.

Just possibly, on one night at one moment, there is in fact not a soul listening.

Does the deejay communicate?

To answer this question we have briefly to examine the nature of communication itself. And as in so many areas of inquiry, nobody comes close to improving upon the communications model devised by Aristotle over two millennia ago. Communication, the ancient master demonstrated with uncanny clarity, requires three components: a Source, a Message, and a Receiver. Without any one of these integral items, communication fails to occur.

The lonely deejay in the remote radio station, therefore, with nobody listening, does not communicate, because there is no receiver for his message. Significantly, of course, he hasn't a clue as to whether anybody is tuned to the program. On blind faith alone he presumes at least a few scattered insomniac jazz buffs are out there, radio dials aglow. He raps his rap, spins his discs, never truly knowing whether his records and impressions are exclusive to himself or actually shared with living, breathing listeners. In either case his behavior is the same. Yet in one instance he communicates and in the other he does not. His ability to communicate does not depend on himself alone but requires also the cooperation, at minimum the existence, of an audience. And that is a curious, painful principle, as he ultimately can only guess whether an audience is there.

Screenwriters operate under similar circumstances. We can characterize the writer as Source, his screenplay as Message, and audience as Receiver. Yet no writer knows with certainty that his script will be produced. This is true even for scripts that are sold, even those sold for substantial sums. It is as true for writers who are wholly unknown as for superstars.

Movie-studio story department shelves are lined with screenplays, commissioned, optioned, purchased, that have yet to be produced. And even among scripts that are produced, many fail to see light of screen as, even after filming, for any of a host of reasons—including plain bad luck—they fail to be exhibited. In such cases, which represent the vast majority of screenwriting experiences, the writers have all the impact they would have had if they had not bothered to write their scripts at all.

Ignoring all of this, screenwriters are compelled to leap a chasm of faith and take as given that what they write is surely to be acted by actors, photographed by cinematographers, edited by editors, and exhibited to audiences. For that, and for other reasons, it's useful for writers to be just a little crazy.

For that, too, it's possible to formulate the screenwriter's first, last, and only commandment: Be worthy of an audience. In other words, the good movie is that which merits the time, attention, and consideration of some collected group of people.

That is screenwriting's lone unbreakable rule: Don't be boring.

Write a movie that, from beginning to end, is merely not boring and people will line up around the block; they will wait patiently outdoors hour after hour through a howling blizzard for the opportunity to trade dollars for the privilege of spending a hundred minutes with the writer's projected fantasy.

But if all that is required of a successful screenplay is to avoid boring an audience, why are there only a hundred or so screenwriters in the entire country (plus perhaps a couple hundred more writing television) who regularly, consistently eke out even a middle-class living? Why aren't there millions more?

How hard can it be, after all, to avoid boredom for a couple of hours?

The answer is plain enough to anyone who has ever struggled to invent a story with characters and context that somehow connect in a seductive way capable of sustaining an audience's interest from eight o'clock until nine-forty.

Writing a good movie—to no small extent writing even a bad movie—is the hardest job there is; for audience-worthiness is a standard every bit as difficult to meet as it is simple to comprehend. Those who have attempted the task appreciate that it is far easier to crank film through a camera than paper through a typewriter.

Yet there are legions who disdain, who positively revile, this simple notion. To acknowledge viewers, they assert, is to pander. To consider audience is to reduce creative expression to prostitution. The authentic artist, they insist, cares not a whit for mere masses. Surely his task is loftier than catering to the lowest common denominator. Fine writers do not calculate whether their work will play in Peoria. They enter a joyful, spiritual trance; they set their creative juices to flowing, their God-gifted imaginations to soaring. And anything they do is beautiful because *they're* beautiful.

But this is, of course, just so much self-worshiping, art-wrecking nonsense.

The burden weighs, in fact, upon the artist to provide for the audience, and not the other way around. Artists who scorn audience, who regard the public with contempt, should here and now renounce all ambition to write for the screen.

An audience may be crowded together in a single theater

or scattered as individuals before countless video screens. It does not have to be the blockbuster crowd that attends *Star Wars*. But neither may it be merely the writer's immediate family and friends.

The screenwriter's basic mission is first of all to divert an assembled mass of civilians from life's natural and inevitable tedium. For if the most we expect from a work of art is that it forever change our lives, the least we may require is that it keep us awake.

Audiences are not stupid. Quite the contrary, evidence abounds that they are smart. If from time to time they embrace works that are superficial and silly, for millennia they have demonstrated also an uncanny knack for recognizing greatness. Since the earliest recorded popular expression, the ancient Greek classics, among works performed and celebrated century after century not one was unknown or unpopular contemporaneously, none was discovered after its time, none failed to reach and affect audiences during its author's lifetime.

Oedipus Rex is no remote, obscure, misplaced work that languished in Sophocles' trunk awaiting the attention of some plucky graduate student in search of a subject for his dissertation. *Hamlet* was not ignored during its own day, finally to be resurrected by modern scholars and critics. Shakespeare's best plays were broad, brawling, blockbuster hits in his own day. From their earliest performances audiences flocked eagerly and repeatedly to see them.

Are there no worthy screenplays that fail to find audiences? Is every hit a good movie and every good movie a hit?

Of course not. Even Aristotle recognized there is such a thing as misfortune. Certainly I do not argue a movie is as good as its audience is large. Picture for picture, the reason particular audiences spark to particular films is forever a mystery.

But no screenwriter need apologize for reaching people. If a work of public and popular expression fails in its own time to find an audience, good or bad as it may well be, it will for all time be lost. And no true artist wishes to be lost.

Conflict: Violence and Sex

Must movies marinate in sex?

No, but many, probably most—including some of the best films ever made—are positively saturated with sensuality and eroticism.

But sex aside, movies must forever be violent. Call it conflict, if you prefer, or tension, or stress. But screenwriters are urgently advised to consider the general disquietude essential to all films as plain, mean, straight-out violence. They are urged also to remember that enlightened, reasonable, rational behavior, combined with courteous agreement, is boring.

This does not require that movie armies perpetually beat out each other's brains. Neither does it insist upon an endless succession of looting and shooting. But there is no escaping the fact that extreme, strident, vigorous, violent emotion must be integrated into each and every frame of each and every scene of each and every movie.

Can a screenplay ever pause, rest, seize a quiet moment for philosophical reflection and tranquil contemplation? It cannot. To paraphrase critic Walter Kerr, in life we kill time; in movies time kills us.

Like it or not, screenwriters come to merit the attention of audiences largely through the skillful shaping and wielding of violence and sex. There's more to movies than that, to be sure, but first of all there is that. Moreover, all the other stuff pales by comparison.

Is this a dark, brooding view? Not at all. It is simply a practical, bare-knuckles approach to the practical, bare-knuckles enterprise that is film.

Film's roots are firmly embedded in theater. Not surprisingly, theater provides plentiful experience from which screenwriters may profit. A careful look at *Oedipus Rex*, for example, cannot harm a writer hoping to know and improve his craft. What's the play all about?

Some say fate, others faith. Still others wax philosophic on the curious qualities of mankind, the peculiar properties of the universe.

None is wholly wrong.

But first and foremost *Oedipus* is about a king who murders his father and beds his mother. It is the story of a fellow who, on different occasions during his lifetime, journeys in both directions through the same birth canal. Then, as if Sophocles feared audiences might find that all just a touch too tame, he ordered his protagonist, upon discovering the sorry truth about his life, not to sigh, not to weep, not to bite his nails or tear his hair or, in a stammering, sobbing soliloquy, otherwise to bemoan his fate. Instead, with sharp metal stakes he pokes out his eyes. Although his deeds were not intentional, he exiles himself from his own land, the land where he is king, to wander in darkness and horror the rest of his wretched days.

What a perverse view of a soaring, timeless classic, scholars and critics might well protest. *Oedipus* contains profound insights into the nature of man and woman. It abounds with poetic lessons treating death's inevitability. It superimposes humankind's powerlessness upon the gods' prescription that in the face of hopelessness each of us struggles to live the moral, fulfilled, and fulfilling life.

Why concentrate merely upon the incest and patricide?

Because unless one is positively bloated with lofty intellect and self-importance, one has to concede that whatever else *Oedipus* treats, first and last it is what it is: a story of a fellow who murders his father and has sexual intercourse with his mother. These features are too glaring to be characterized as only incidental to whatever else the play also offers.

Likewise *Hamlet*, for all its poetry and grace, its rich characters and effectively crafted story, is a tale of sex, greed, and death. By final curtain the stage is awash with blood, littered with no fewer than nine corpses. Bodies are run through on swords, others poisoned.

Next to *Medea,* however, these two tales are *Bambi.*

Medea, in a jealous rage engendered by her husband's faithlessness, not only murders her children but cooks and serves them to their father for dinner. Imagine pitching such a project to the story department of a movie studio. "Disgusting!" the executive vice presidents would surely exclaim. "We'll have every parent group in the country picketing our offices, burning down our theaters. Senate committees will audit our books. Bloodthirsty mobs will lynch our projectionists!"

Let me concede again eagerly, even gratefully, that violence in movies does not need precisely to be blood-and-guts gore. Still, among the best loved classics it is almost invariably just that.

But what of artists' social responsibility?

Responsible movies and television should also, ultimately, promote nourishing, constructive behavior. Attempting from the start to serve lofty moral and social purposes is a recipe for failure. It leads film and television artists to succeed not in achieving their noble objectives but only in boring their audience. A warm, well-intentioned film bearing the unfortunate title, *Amazing Grace and Chuck*, attempted from the first frame to arouse audiences to the threat of atomic annihilation and the need for straight-thinking common folk to become actively involved in opposing the proliferation of nuclear weapons. These are decent, honorable intentions, to be sure, but can the cause of world peace truly be served by a remote, speechy, preachy, self-important film? In all history there is not a single instance in which tedious obscurity is known to have uplifted anybody or served any good purpose.

Screenwriters serve society best by struggling to provide worthwhile shows for living, breathing, flesh-and-blood audiences.

But do not sociopaths and psychopaths imitate the violence they view on screen?

It may well seem so, but in fact there is no scientific evidence that this is true. Studies establishing a causal relationship between media and violence win grants from foundations but tend to be flawed. Generally they derive from the logical fallacy of *post hoc, ergo propter hoc*—"after this, therefore *because* of this." If one thing follows another, the second had to be caused by the first.

These days anyone in America can prove he is an instant genius—one imbued with social responsibility—by denouncing film and television and firmly affixing to it a causal relationship with everything that is wrong with the nation and the world.

When I was growing up, all the world's evils were blamed on comic books.

Today it's television.

I preach here not that violence is desirable, but merely that it is a natural and inevitable quality of public and popular expression. To take film and television to task for violence is like criticizing rivers for flowing downstream.

The violent nature of film can be appreciated or deplored, addressed or ignored, but it is relentlessly present. Conflict permeates every worthy play, film, and television program.

Earlier, by way of illustration, I compared *Oedipus Rex, Hamlet,* and *Medea* to the tranquil *Bambi.*

But consider even *Bambi*! A positively adorable fawn—is there any other kind?—witnesses her own doe-eyed mother shot to death by hunters. She flees a raging forest fire. Orphaned, she wanders the forest alone in creeping, cringing terror.

The classic Disney productions, movie for movie, are perhaps the most consistently horrific among all films. And each of them aimed directly at children!

One Hundred and One Dalmations, as another example, is a uniquely mean-spirited, perverse tale. An evil witch abducts scores of cuddly puppies in order to skin them alive and wear their pelts as a coat!

We may like it, we may loathe it, but surely we must face

the fact: Extreme, marked, deeply etched, vigorously underscored conflict—call it violence—is a natural and inevitable property of film and television.

Having said that, let me now assert also that violence in films need not be physical at all. It is more than sufficient for the conflict to be psychological, spiritual, emotional. From that standpoint *Kramer vs. Kramer* is among the more violent films of recent years. Yet here is a film in which neither flesh nor bone are abused.

In *Kramer vs. Kramer,* the most grievous physical trauma occurs mid-picture, when the young son suffers a fall in the playground. Cradling the boy in his arms, the father, portrayed by Dustin Hoffman, sprints several blocks to the hospital.

Happily, the injury turns out to be superficial.

Nevertheless, *Kramer vs. Kramer* is an extraordinarily violent film. What could be more violent than a mother and father battling for the custody of their flesh-and-blood offspring? What could be more heartbreaking than the battle for the living, breathing issue of what once must have been their transcendent love?

Again, many may characterize this kind of violence as mere conflict.

And again, I urge film and television writers to see it for what it truly is: violence. Such a view encourages more vigorous application. And the broader, the more pronounced it is, the more closely are audiences drawn to it. Every scene, every moment in every movie thirsts for identifiable conflict. A responsible screenwriter can point to any section of his script and precisely answer the question: Where is the conflict?

The best intentions of the highest-minded practitioners aside, violence and sex are whole, natural, necessary ingredients in television and film. No screenwriter has to apologize for soaking his script with toe-to-toe, eyeball-to-eyeball conflict—social conflict, emotional conflict, spiritual conflict, cultural conflict, psychological conflict, and, yes, physical conflict too—scene for scene, page for page.

Airplanes that land safely do not make the news. And nobody goes to the theater, or switches on the tube, to view a movie entitled *The Village of the Happy Nice People.*

Credibility: What Is Real and What Is Reel

Movies are fake.

For one thing, they don't even move. A typical feature-length film is actually some hundred and fifty thousand individual still photographs projected in rapid succession upon a blank screen. Since there are twenty-four such frames per second, it seems sensible to calculate that each frame plays on the screen for one twenty-fourth portion of a second.

Yet even this is not true.

The engineers who designed motion picture projectors integrated into the mechanism a shutter that revolves once each cycle in order to block the light during pull-down, masking the film's mechanical motion through the gate. Between every single projected transparency, therefore, sharing the cycle with the lighted frame is a period of total darkness. And the darkness between frames consumes a shade more time than the frame itself. In other words, projected film consists mainly of blackness. During a typical feature running a hundred minutes, the shutter is closed cumulatively for an entire hour.

The mechanics and engineering of motion-picture projection underscore a most fundamental screenwriting principle: *Life is real, and film is contrivance.* Film is, in fact, as contrived an enterprise as is possible for the human mind to imagine.

A preposterous exaggeration?

Exaggeration for effect is a perfectly legitimate screenwriting tool. Nevertheless, I exaggerate here not in the least. For what could be more arranged, manipulated, ordered, crafted, shuffled, and reshuffled than the elements of a movie? Time, space, story, and characters are configured and reconfigured at the writer's will and convenience. Actors, in many cases already well-known to audiences for the people they truly are, pretend to be characters they clearly are not. They strut about in situations that are orchestrated right down to makeup, hair, wardrobe, and light. They recite memorized dialogue acknowledged to have been written by writers. Yet, if the actors capably own their craft, and if the writing is good, they deliver the lines in such manner as to convey the notion that they thought the words up all by themselves, that the ideas just happened to occur to them at the moment they spoke them. Similarly, the actors move about the frame as if, without plan or prearrangement, they stumbled naturally into the circumstances depicted on the screen. What is carefully staged and rehearsed is presented as if it were spontaneous.

Moreover, as even the most superficial student of film craft appreciates, scenes in films do not unfold on screen in the same order as they are photographed. Some scenes, photographed earlier, appear later; others, filmed later, appear earlier. Even some substantial portion of the dialogue is likely to have been recorded—and rerecorded—in different places and at separate times.

View a film, therefore, and you look at a broken-up, disjointed, disconnected assemblage of bits and pieces of scattered shots. The miracle is that they seem to flow smoothly in an orderly fashion, permitting us to believe that we peer into real people's real lives, although we know precisely the opposite is the case, that the entire construction is one giant pretense.

Naturally, audiences ought never consciously realize this condition of a particular film as they watch it. But since there's a marquee over the entrance to the theater, since they bought tickets, since they're chomping popcorn and Milk Duds, somewhere inside their subconscious they must surely realize the whole enterprise is one elaborate shuck-and-jive. And surely the last thing they desire or deserve is the truth.

Truth is available in the street outside the theater for

free. Nobody has to hire a babysitter, nobody has to hunt around for a parking place, nobody has to wait in line in the snow, nobody has to shell out six dollars for the privilege of passing a hundred minutes with reality. It is not truth but sweet, seductive falsehood that audiences crave.

Bluntly stated, the screenwriter's mission is skillfully and lovingly to lie.

Yet among screenwriters, especially among inexperienced screenwriters, there is a self-destructive compulsion to be truthful. Surely this has to do with the most fundamental nature of film itself, its technology, its tradition.

When Thomas Edison invented the kinetoscope, upon what did he train its lens? On anything that moved. Do you invent a motion-picture machine to record objects standing still?

Edison's first films are of nothing besides motion—the carriages, the streetcars, the pedestrians striding down the street outside his workshop/studio. Soon enough scores of early cinematographers were capturing images of trains barreling down the track, waterfalls roaring over high cliffs, indigenous peoples in their natural climes, prominent political personalities cutting ribbons, launching ships, delivering speeches in total silence. For years mere motion was enough to fascinate audiences, until, at around the turn of the century, filmmakers for the first time found it necessary to synthesize actions and events, to arrange incidents and anecdotes into some semblance of order so as to hold an audience's attention, even if only for several minutes.

It was at this moment that screenwriting was born.

Surely it is film's early roots in recording reality, combined with the camera's portability—its capacity to re-create scenes in their natural locations instead of on stages as in theater—that explain at least in part movie writers' obsession with verisimilitude.

Granted, much of moviemaking occurs today not on location but at studios on soundstages, but no one who ever wandered through a dressed set has failed to be astounded by the faith with which reality is faked. A Harlem street on a back lot, populated with appropriately costumed extras, looks exactly like the real thing. A middle-American home looks like a middle-American home. A medieval castle looks like a medieval castle. And if the set, the props, the people seem so real up close, consider how vastly enhanced is that authenticity when removed one generation via cinematography. For the movie camera is a miraculous device, allowing representations of things that appear somehow even more real than those things they represent.

Recently I had a meeting at Columbia Pictures, one of two major movie companies at The Burbank Studios in Southern California. From there I walked over to Warner Brothers, also located at the Burbank facility, in order to gossip with pals. Between the Columbia and Warner offices lies the studio back-lot setting of, among others, a midwestern American town square.

It was a paralyzingly hot day in mid-July, unusual even for Burbank, with the mercury at one hundred and fourteen degrees.

The midwestern street on that day happened to be dressed for winter; a dry white powder had been blown copiously but carefully throughout the area, sculpted into bogus drifts against cars, on porches and eaves. Precise tire tracks were carved into the simulated snow, and translucent vinyl icicles hung from window ledges and rain gutters.

Even firsthand, even without photography's mysterious ability to mask, the effect was so genuine that right there on the hottest day of the year I shivered and secured my collar more tightly about my neck! The vigorous suggestion of cold was more than sufficient to evoke an authentic chill.

Credit where due: Here is one area where the Hollywood film community, for all its shortcomings, performs with consistent magnificence. Say what you will about mainstream movies, one quantity Hollywood always delivers is a high-grade look, a blinding facsimile of reality.

It is not reality but this facsimile of reality to which

screenwriters must aspire. For real, true stories with real, true characters generally tend to offend screenwriting's first principle: They are boring. Truth, it is frequently asserted, is stranger than fiction. And undoubtedly once in a while this is actually the case.

But in fact, far more often truth is relentlessly, numbingly dull. It is the day-to-day annoyances, errands, chores we all face. And while an audience's lives outside the movie theater may from time to time be rife with astonishment, more often than not—*much* more often—they are a swarm with petty details like taxes, sniffles, rashes, squabbles, bruises, broken shoelaces, a host of experiences we would gladly forgo.

Whose life is perpetually inspiring, invigorating, exciting, expanding, eye-opening? Nobody's. Even the President of the United States goes to the bathroom, argues with his wife, reads lengthy reports rampant with details he could live without.

Life is in its nature positively saturated with tedium.

And thank goodness for it!

For without it, there would be no need for art, for creative expression of any kind including movies. And that would be a terrible pity, since good films are expanding, life-affirming experiences that explain to us in some small way where, who, why we are. When they become preoccupied with a petty, ill-considered devotion to superficial figures and facts, they betray their true calling.

Beware, therefore, of movies that purport to tell the truth.

Philosophers, intellectuals, artists, poets, scientists have argued for millennia about the nature of truth. And so it is reasonable to be skeptical of anyone who claims finally to have it all figured out.

For if truth is always to be sought, it is never to be known.

Victor Weiskopf, Nobel laureate physicist and mathematician, suggests there are actually two kinds of truth: superficial truth and profound truth. The first kind is truth the opposite of which is untrue. The latter is truth the opposite of which is somehow *also* true.

And such is the truth we seek in art. Truth of this order involves more than knowing precisely how many beans are in the jar.

Historical, factual, scientific research has its place, to be sure, but too often among screenwriters it is utilized *instead* of writing. Serious writers learn quickly that it is easier to spend hours, even months, combing through books and journals, conducting interviews, compiling data, and recording footnotes, than to sit alone in a room with blank paper or glowing green phosphor, employing only thought and language, struggling to construct from thin air a tale with rich, ripe characters speaking naturalistic yet poetic dialogue worthy of troubling some assembled mass of people.

The challenge for screenwriters is not to look it up but to make it up.

PART II
NUTS AND BOLTS

3

STORY:

Tale Assembly

Story is to movies as melody to music.

To be sure, there is more to music than melody. Rhythm, tempo, texture, and tone are among a host of elements. But first comes melody. And melody is by far the most elusive, the most difficult component to achieve. It is much easier to devise an engaging beat, for example, or a unique texture, or an affecting tone, than to construct a melodic line starting somewhere, naturally and inevitably flowing somewhere else, pausing here to breathe, moving now to the next station on its own seductive, hypnotic continuum, and arriving, finally, somewhere the listener acknowledges in his heart is the one place it positively must go.

A tale, no doubt apocryphal, is told of the young Mozart. Like most teenagers, he liked to sleep late. And like most teenagers' mothers, Frau Mozart forever nagged him to arise. On a particular day when he was especially reluctant to stir, she conceived a brilliant notion. Instead of poking his ribs and scolding, she hurried downstairs to the harpsichord and played an incomplete scale: do, re, mi, fa, so, la, ti . . .

Ti . . . ?

The sequence hung motionless in the air, aching to be resolved. The tension had to be relieved, the score settled.

The octave had resoundingly to be struck. Anybody with ears would have been eager for the resolution of that incomplete scale, but for one so keenly attuned as young Wolfgang it represented a special agony.

He leaped from bed, took the stairs four at a time and struck the final, calming "doooo," sighing, no doubt, with monumental relief.

Story craft is no different. Something happens—instead of a note call it an anecdote, incident, or event. Its immediate result is a sweetly painful tension, which in turn compels something else—yet another incident or event—to follow. This tension/relief Ping-Pong game lies at the heart of story craft.

Many inexperienced screenwriters labor under a destructive illusion. Denigrating story, believing they possess instead a special knack for, say, creating fascinating characters, they convince themselves that to launch a script they need merely recall their creaking, cranky third-grade teacher, their crazy prankster pal from the old neighborhood, their quirky, affectionate mother, their high school swim coach, their high school swim coach's quirky, affectionate mother. They expect the other details of the script somehow to sort themselves out.

Still other new writers believe that while they may not have a particular lock on character, they are God's gift to dialogue. They own an uncanny ear with a distinct penchant for the natural, gritty, authentic poetry spoken by real people in real situations.

They do not doubt for a second that ripe settings populated with rich characters expressing crisp, nifty dialogue will carry a movie.

Few writers, however, boast of a solid story sense. None—among them the world's most experienced, successful practitioners—maintains that story comes smoothly, effortlessly, without struggle.

In the recent past, story, typically belittled as "narrative," came to be characterized—to no small extent like writing itself—as outmoded, linear, constricting. Narrative, we heard repeatedly from every quarter, serves only to stifle true creativity, to suffocate effective character development.

Untested writers, and no small number of pop theoreticians, insisted that story is no more than a mail-order catalogue of incidents: this happens; that happens; something else happens after that. It was suggested that liberated writers could dispense with story altogether. They had merely to patch together a bunch of good characters, plop them in exotic, original settings, stick bright, brittle banter in their collective craw, and a story would shape itself.

The reality is, however, that stories do not shape themselves. Writers shape stories. It is no accident that the motion picture studio office dealing with writers is not called the idea department, nor the theme department, nor the dialogue department, nor the character department. It is called the Story Department.

While all the elements of a screenplay are important, and none exists independently of any other, the most important component of all, and certainly the most difficult to craft, is story.

The three most important facets of story craft are: (1) structure; (2) structure; (3) structure.

Alas, it is especially difficult for the lay person—indeed, for the vast majority of experienced writers—to comprehend precisely what *structure* signifies when applied to story. The structure of a house is easy enough. There are a whole host of elements embodied in a house, but the basic structure includes three items: floor, walls, roof.

A story, on the other hand, upon first glance appears nothing at all like a house. A house is a tangible, measurable entity. You can stand beside it; you can stand within it; you can stand upon it. You can run your hand over portions of it, stroll through and around it, regard it from any number of vantages.

Story, however, represents a construct whose nature is internal, intellectual, emotional. It is made up not of beams but of thoughts, built not of bricks but of words. It can be read aloud so that one may hear it. But it cannot truly be seen, except inside one's own head—until, of course, it happens to illuminate a movie screen.

Still, while a story is in so many ways different from a house, like a house it has a clearly identifiable structure. And like a house its basic structural components are threefold.

They are: (1) beginning; (2) middle; (3) end.

This notion, the three-part model of story structure, was first articulated nearly twenty-five hundred years ago by Aristotle.

As evidence of Aristotle's wisdom through the centuries, no one has truly improved upon his model. This testifies not to the weakness of Aristotle's successors, but rather to the awesome nature of what may seem at first glance to be a simplistic vision.

The beginning of a story, Aristotle tells us, is that part which comes first, and before which is nothing.

The middle, it follows, follows.

What the middle follows, you may already have guessed, is the beginning.

The middle itself is followed, also predictably, by the end.

And the end is followed by nothing.

Let us promptly confront an obvious truth: This model may appear so obvious, so glaringly self-evident, as to seem quite useless.

To be sure, the notion has been around far too long to be considered anything like revolutionary. But a theory need not be new to be worthy; it need merely prove practical. And the trick to utilizing Aristotle's story model is to embrace it not in an ethereal, philosophical fashion but quite the contrary, as a seat-of-the-pants, nuts-and-bolts approach to screen story construction.

Aristotle's *Poetics*, if you take the time to read it (as I vigorously recommend), ought to be embraced as the classical equivalent of *How to Clean the Carburetor of Your Honda Civic*. Consider it history's first self-help, how-to, career-change, bootstrap mass text. It deserves, more particularly it requires, the most painstaking, step-by-step consideration. It need not be interpreted at all; it needs simply be followed.

A good place to start is the beginning. And what is important to remember about the beginning is not so much that it comes first but that it is that part *before which there is nothing*.

Again, this might seem self-evident. Does not every school child appreciate that the beginning of anything is preceded by nothing?

Yet in my experience reading thousands of screenplays by amateurs and professionals alike, perhaps the single most common error is screenwriters' failure to begin at the beginning. Sometimes, rarely, screenplays start after the beginning. But all too typically they commence *before* the beginning.

Kramer vs. Kramer is an example of a film that begins at its proper beginning. At the picture's opening, Mrs. Kramer, capably portrayed by Meryl Streep, stands in the doorway, bags packed, trying to impress upon her husband that she is leaving, that their marriage is over.

A less skillful screenwriter likely would have gone back to the couple's college days, their meeting, courting, marriage. There would follow a point-by-point description detailing the relationship's steady decline. He squeezes the toothpaste in the middle of the tube; it enrages her. She wrings out her panties in the sink and leaves them draped over the porcelain lip; it disgusts him. His career soars and he's out late servicing his accounts; she grows morose whiling away the lonely hours watching soaps, neglecting child, snorting whiskey and cocaine. Eventually, perhaps by the end of Act II, some seventy or eighty pages into the script, an hour and a quarter into the picture, they are at each other's throat. She weeps over his lack of affection. He gripes about her lack of career support. She threatens to leave. He calls her bluff. And at long last her bags are packed, she's out the door.

But screenwriter/adaptor Robert Benton knows the tale is not that of husband and wife but father and son; it is a story not of separation (man/spouse) but of reconciliation (parent/child).

The boy and man start out as virtual strangers, isolated from each other by the father's narcissistic preoccupation with career. The script commences properly, therefore, with mother, bags packed, standing in the doorway. What went sour in the marriage is not pertinent. This is not to suggest that a rocky marriage could not be the subject of a film; it is merely not this film.

In *Kramer vs. Kramer* the end of the marriage is the beginning of the picture. Recognizing this, commencing at the authentic beginning, not a frame is wasted. Mom is jettisoned right at the start; father and son are promptly, properly hurled together at the absolute beginning.

Writers are well advised constantly to ask themselves of the beginning of their tale: Is this the true beginning? Is this the point before which there is nothing? What would be lost if I started on page eight? Or eleven? Twenty-two? If nothing would be lost by starting on page eleven, start there. If starting on page twenty-two would merely cause some scattered but crucial information to be lost, perhaps that data can be inserted strategically somewhere into the succeeding pages, relocated in the context of a particular character's speech, replaced by a definitive action by one or another player. Conveying some random information does not justify beginning a story twenty-two pages before its proper beginning.

Indeed, the question *is this the true beginning?* can be applied not only to a script but even more precisely to a particular scene, or more narrowly still, to a single line of dialogue.

If a scene takes place in a restaurant, for example (bearing in mind that wherever possible scenes in restaurants are to be avoided—see Chapter 6, "Action and Setting"), one need not show the principals arriving, greeted, being seated. No audience need observe the distribution of the menus.

Neither do people buy tickets to films in order to hear cocktails ordered, wine selected, tasted, served. Since movies can cut right to the middle (technically the beginning) of an action or event, they *must* do precisely that—skip the menus, cocktails, wine, and leap directly to the meat of the scene. If one absolutely cannot avoid setting a scene in a restaurant, then the scene ought to open with the characters already present, seated, and served, and get right down to the pertinent, story-moving, character-advancing business at hand.

Structure is not limited merely to broad questions concerning story. Even a single line of dialogue is worthy of examination in order to determine whether it begins at the beginning. As emphasized in Chapter 5, "Dialogue," one need never open a line with "Look," or "Listen," or "Well," for no matter what follows is already starting after that point before which nothing is needed. The test, of course, is simply to eliminate the suspect beginning, and decide whether any truly significant information is lost. Is there any worthy difference between "Look, I love you" and "I love you?"

Granted, widely scattered instances of "Look," "Listen," or "Say," won't all by themselves wreck a script, but collectively they take the edge off the tale's thrust, blunting its momentum. Subliminally, they signal both the script's readers and the film's viewers that rigorous economy is not observed by this writer, that he does not truly value their time. A failure to observe economy in one area inevitably manifests itself in every other corner of his screenplay. The script brimming with unnecessary introductions and interjections invariably also contains lines and even whole scenes that can be excised.

Responsible creative expression requires that anything that *can* be excised *must* be excised. If it is not truly needed, why squander an audience's time?

More broadly, writers can view story from the vantage of the nature of the universe itself. Shatter an object into its smallest parts and discover that those fragments bear an uncanny resemblance to the whole grand scheme. The infinitesimally small atom, for example, with its electrons circling its nucleus, reminds us of the structure of the whole solar system, with the planets circling the sun.

Or consider the hologram, a laser-produced, three-dimensional photo. Unlike the standard photographic negative, the hologram's "negative," when cut in half, continues somehow to reproduce the whole picture. This is because even just a fraction of the whole contains the entire interference pattern—which is the hologram's root—for the complete original image.

This is merely another way of suggesting that little things look like big things.

Writers should constantly note that residing within the smallest part of any one movie is a reflection of the whole picture, exactly as every cell in our bodies contains in its DNA all the genetic information necessary to reproduce the entire body.

To state it more simply, as whole movies have structures encompassing beginnings, middles, and ends, so also do parts of movies—scenes, actions, dialogue, to name a few.

This is not just loose philosophical rambling, but a concrete, pragmatic strategy for improving scenes, actions, snatches of dialogue, and entire screenplays. It can go a long way toward helping a writer identify his movie's structure, and it can alert him to irrelevant parts that must be discarded. This is critically important to effective writing, because any part of a movie that has no purpose has no purpose being there.

It is the same for all creative activity, even, for example, the design of a console belonging to a top-of-the-line automobile. Say that a particular dial is the tachometer. Imagine that a certain lever engages overdrive. Assume that there is a rotational rheostat to activate the windshield wipers.

But wait. What's that little toggle over there? Oh, it serves no function, it's not connected to anything. So why is it there? No particular reason; the designer just felt like including it. Perhaps he thinks it looks pretty, perhaps he likes the crisp, resonant click it emits when moved from one setting to the next. Perhaps the decision to include it came to him in a religious vision.

Clearly, such a designer would soon find himself out of a job, and deservedly so. No artist can creatively integrate an element just for a giggle; fun as it may prove, each item needs to belong. Each requires its special place. Each must fulfill a precise, identifiable function.

In screenplays as in automobiles, form and function occupy no adversarial relationship but instead are inextricably integrated into each other. Ideally, as in all artistic expression, everything fits; every facet, every component has a precise and proper purpose.

Writers truly grasping this fundamental principle can devise smart structural strategies that help shake loose the barnacles from their screenplays. A wholly integrated beginning/middle/end mind-set vastly economizes screenwriting, from dialogue through larger scenes to full stories.

It is worthwhile, therefore, to review some specific rules pertinent to the three-part model of tale assembly.

First (appropriately), beginnings.

Beginnings

A proper beginning for a screenplay, difficult as it may be to attain, is a relatively easy matter compared to middles and ends. The world positively abounds with people claiming grand film openings for which the middles and ends remain to be thought up, much less written down. I have yet to hear, however, from a single person who has no beginning or middle, but nevertheless possesses somehow a fabulous conclusion to a one-day-to-be-written film.

It is far easier to spin the various threads belonging to a particular tale than to weave those same strands into a beautifully integrated knot of an ending.

Beyond that, writers simply are not likely to show only

their beginnings to anyone; the tendency is (wisely) to wait until the script is finished. No script's reader, therefore, can ridicule merely a writer's beginning, since no writer is likely to submit the beginning alone for consideration.

Perhaps that is among the reasons writers often dash off beginnings but crawl like snails through endings.

The key to beginnings, to reiterate, is to start as Aristotle prescribes, at that point before which no information is required. *Citizen Kane* starts at what appears to be the end, Kane's death, but this is promptly seen to be the genuine beginning, as the biographical tale now flashes back to his earliest childhood, that same childhood reflected in the snowy crystal ball that opens the film. In *Grapes of Wrath* the same moment is found in Tom Joad's return from prison to the abandoned family homestead. We don't need to see him in jail; we don't even need to know why he was incarcerated in the first place. We only need to realize he has come home to discover he has no home.

It is extremely important for film writers to recognize that structure is not formula, despite the tendency among film educators to wax formulaic when discussing story shape. To integrate the scattered elements of a screen story is different from assembling a tricycle from its shipping crate. There is more to writing a screenplay than fastening flange A to tab B, and securing strut C with wing nut D. Although script structure most assuredly adheres to certain immutable laws, the miracle is that screenplays are at the same time as individual as the writers who write them.

Primary among these rules is that the three basic parts— beginning, middle, end—are not equal in size. Beginnings, for example, are sometimes shorter than endings and sometimes not. But both beginnings and endings are invariably shorter than middles.

In the beginning of any screenplay certain obvious tasks need to be addressed. But they are addressed not because writers consciously resolve to address them. Instead, they are irrevocably integrated into the nature of beginning.

Primary among these tasks are establishing the movie's

tone, introducing the protagonist, and presenting any necessary exposition.

Tone

A film's tone—comedic, tragic, melodramatic—needs to be consistent.

More often than not, when differing tones seep into each others' territories, it is only testimony to the writer's failure to resolve the challenge of story structure. Too frequently a film that has been texturally serious, gritty, down-and-dirty for the vast bulk of its length suddenly toward the end dissolves into silliness. Almost inevitably it fools no one. Audiences will not tolerate a failure of story craft, an inability to shape a well-rounded tale, by suddenly turning everything into a big, broad joke. It is the transparent equivalent of setting up some impossible situation and then paying it off by having the protagonist wake up to discover it was all a dream.

To achieve a smartly finessed stylistic crossover requires the true genius of a writer like Terry Southern collaborating with a formidable director like Stanley Kubrick. And it requires also no small quantity of luck. In *Dr. Strangelove*, for example, we have an absurd, slapstick comedy defiantly integrated with a terrifyingly believable military adventure. And no doubt it is the comedy's special blackness superimposed upon the suitably grim tale of nuclear holocaust that renders the combination acceptable.

But a *Dr. Strangelove* is exceptional. Tone more commonly requires quite the opposite: precise, rock-steady evenhandedness and consistency from start to finish.

I have already said that a film's tone needs to be established at its beginning. It is nonetheless a mistake for writers to decide in advance precisely what the tone will be. Rather, it emerges in the context of working on the specific script. Should a writer have a vague notion to write a thriller, for example, only to discover it is shaping up as substantially comedic, he is mistaken to insist upon establishing the originally intended tone. This leads all too easily to locking the tale into a stylistic straitjacket. Instead, the writer should allow the script to assert its own tone, which, after all is said and done, is nothing less than a reflection of his own personality, talent, and capabilities.

Once a writer finds his story's tone, whatever it may be, and surprising as it may prove even to the writer himself, that tone needs constantly to be maintained.

Introducing the Protagonist

The nature of a movie's protagonist proves the ultimate falseness of dissecting a screenplay into disparate components as if these distinct items truly existed independently of one another.

It might very well appear that the proper place to discuss the protagonist, as an example, is the chapter on character. But in fact when we talk about a tale's protagonist, we treat not just another character in the film, nor even merely the film's central player.

We treat, instead, a basic tenet of story structure.

Ideally, the protagonist is the singular identity within the film. Sometimes the role of protagonist is shared by two or more characters. And here is where problems arise. For the wider the sharing, the softer the focus of the entire film.

Collective protagonists are by nature a genuine hazard to solid story structure. Lawrence Kasdan's *The Big Chill* is all too perfect an example. The focus of his otherwise admirable tale is so democratic, spread so evenly over the half-dozen collected central characters, that the tale is forced to move indiscriminately from one player to the next, reminding us of the old saw: "We don't discriminate here; we treat *everybody* badly."

Artists *need* to discriminate. That's their job as surely as a bus driver's job is to drive a bus. To discriminate is to choose. And creative choice is art's nature. With screenwriting, the choices are word after word, scene after scene. And it is precisely from this endless succession of hard choices that a script's characters and dialogue and all its other qualities derive.

It is not impossible to craft an effective ensemble piece, one treating a collective group, and still somehow eventually identify a clear protagonist. *American Graffiti* is an example. Here screenwriters George Lucas, Willard Huyck, and Gloria Katz succeed in establishing four central figures who are treated in what appears for the most part to be an evenhanded fashion. Yet long before the film's end it is quite clear that the character portrayed by Richard Dreyfuss is in fact the film's true center. His voice represents that of the author.

For its failure to manifest the same clear choice, *The Big Chill* spreads itself too thin. As soon as we begin to learn of a particular character's desires and disappointments we are whisked away to yet another player without a true chance fully to consider the first.

Would not *The Big Chill* have worked far more effectively had the writer chosen one or another member to play the central role? It could have been the young dancer, girlfriend of the deceased. Certainly this would have permitted the old college chums to be viewed from a singular vantage; it would have allowed for the kind of counterpoint—youngster against oldsters (or "middle"-sters), or sixties culture versus eighties culture—that brings characters and stories and themes into physical relief.

Another tactic would have been to assign the role of protagonist to the couple—portrayed by Glenn Close and Kevin Kline—at whose house the action plays out. Perhaps, since spreading the protagonist over even only two people causes the focus to blur, it could have been solely Glenn Close herself. In either instance a clearer dramatization of the marriage, stable relationships versus unstable relationships, the very nature of relationship itself, could have been explored and evaluated in a tale enjoying a sharper, more direct thrust.

Then again, the role of protagonist could as easily have resided in the figure portrayed by William Hurt. For me the film only comes fully to life at that point at the dinner table when Hurt protests that the group's close-knittedness is a sham, a shared narcissistic illusion. Far from dear, longtime friends, he insists they are in fact strangers who once, many years in the past, knew each other briefly. Here, at last, arrives an opportunity to confront loyalty, disloyalty, the nature of friendship itself.

Instead, in yet another attempt to service every player fairly, Kasdan moves on to the next character, allotting him his own five minutes as "guest" protagonist before the joint is passed once again to yet another equally deserving figure.

Everybody gets treated fairly, except for the audience.

Each movie needs its protagonist with clear needs, and hurdles obstructing the path to satisfying those needs. And that character, those needs, those hurdles, and that tone must be asserted in the film's beginning.

Time Lock

Often, usually early in a script, a clever screenwriter plants a time lock, a structural device requiring some specific event to occur, or some particular problem to be resolved, within a clearly predetermined period of time. This serves to compress the story's tension.

In *The Bridge on the River Kwai* it is established early that the bridge not only needs to be built but also must be completed by a certain date. This hurries the film's conclusion. Under any circumstances the bridge's destruction is a splendid climax. But the time lock lends sweet perfection not to the end alone but to the entire tale. It is just that much more delicious to have the bridge finished in the nick of time for the train's arrival, and just in time, also, for the explosion that sends bridge and train crashing into the river hundreds of feet below.

In *36 Hours* the time lock is still more inextricably integrated into the tale's structure. The invasion of Europe is but days away; the Nazis have precious little time to extract from James Garner its schedule and location. Sure, without the time lock the effective methods for seducing Garner into revealing the information would play quite well, but the lock device lends the picture both tension and balance. It provides the tale with its shape, a Swiss watch movement in which all the pieces rock up and back in consonant unison, resulting in motion that is consistently forward.

Not all stories lend themselves to time locks, but the resourceful writer digs deeply to locate a method and a place for crafting one into a script.

Exposition

The term *exposition* derives from *expose*. This suggests not creating new facts but revealing information already present but not yet available to viewers.

Too often exposition entails a man with a pointer standing before a map pronouncing some version of: "We have three divisions to complete three missions in three days; the Japanese emplacements are here; our troops are here. The aircraft will strafe here. Landing craft will hit the shore here."

Even the most mundane film wants more invention and imagination.

Exposition is necessary at the start of virtually every film. Writers should keep it short, present it in a fresh manner, and avoid making more of it than it is worth.

The best way to address exposition is to spit it out, get it over with, move along.

In *Stand by Me* the exposition is handled rather self-consciously via a heavily pensive, ever-so-serious Richard Dreyfuss portraying The Writer. In a voice-of-doom narration he spells out for the audience events that transpired years ago. And he prepares the viewers (as if it were necessary to do so) for the film to follow.

In *American Graffiti* the exposition is far more efficiently addressed. It is launched with little more than a dully lighted radio dial and music. In a flash the time, place, and circumstances are set. Soon, in a handful of quick exchanges we learn that Howard and Dreyfuss are planning to leave town in the morning.

Perhaps the most inventive "man-with-a-pointer" exposition in recent years belongs to the British film *Local Hero*, in which a captain of industry addresses a gathered group of industrial bigwigs in a corporate board room. Standing before the map of a Scottish port, he wields the proverbial pointer, describing this aspect and that aspect of the coast's topography. What is different about this scene? The biggest of the wigs, portrayed by Burt Lancaster, is fast asleep. What is more, none of the sycophantic underlings dares disturb him. The scene is played out, therefore, with all the characters whispering. It lends a cocky edge to the scene and renders what ought to appear deadly dull instead fresh and funny.

A similarly clever twist is employed in the little-seen *Silver Bears* starring Michael Caine. A group of old mafiosi strip naked, don plush bathrobes, march down a penthouse corridor high above Las Vegas. They enter a vast, round, steaming, bubbling therapy pool, discard their robes and— two-foot-long cigars clamped firmly in their teeth—settle into the water.

There now follows what otherwise would be the all too familiar obligatory Mafia boardroom scene. The one change, however, moving it from a richly paneled corporate board room to a tiled, steamy hot tub and turning the players into fat old naked men, makes it different from all the other films burdened with this same scene.

However it is accomplished, once the exposition is exposed, and once an audience appreciates a film's environment and tone, and once an obstacle is thrown rudely into the protagonist's path, we are ready to take a sharp turn toward the Middle.

Middles

Some theoreticians characterize endings as the hardest part of the three-component structure model. They are wrong. The hardest part of a screenplay is the middle.

For one thing, the middle is the longest of the three parts, constituting the tale's true bulk; it is several times larger than the beginning and the end combined.

But length alone is not the primary reason the middle is hardest.

I already have suggested why beginnings are relatively easy. Every writer, by the time he has finished outlining his story and finally sits down to write the script, fairly well appreciates how it begins. Further, he most likely has a definite notion as to how and where it will conclude. To be sure, if he is wise he will prepare himself for changes and surprises, and more to the point, he will *allow* those changes and surprises to flow without hauling the script back to some preordained scheme that may no longer effectively serve him or his audience.

Just before the middle, just at the end of the beginning, stories typically seem smooth, uncomplicated. The reporters agree that "Rosebud" is the key to Kane's life; they'll conduct interviews and figure it all out. Tom Joad catches up with his family, they resolve to seek a new life in California, and all will be hunky-dory. British officer Alec Guinness wins his point with the Japanese prison camp commandant; the latter will respect the former's rank, the former will build a fine, sturdy bridge crossing the River Kwai right on schedule. In *American Graffiti*, Richard Dreyfuss and Ron Howard will enjoy a final, riotous, fun-filled night in their hometown and move away to greater glory. In *Captains Courageous* the rich young spoiled brat is rescued from the drink by the humble Portuguese fisherman who will quickly, smoothly return him to his proper station.

But audiences are not fools. They know the movie can't end after only ten or twelve minutes. That alone ought to be enough to signal that complications are in store for both themselves and the characters in the film they are viewing. If the beginning launches the tale, in the middle the plot thickens. Obstacles arise.

Indeed, some commentators assert that the only way to create a taut yarn is for the writer to place the protagonist here, his goal there, and then to litter his path with every obstacle imaginable. There is a bit more craft required than simply that, but even all by itself it is no mean view of the story-making process.

Inevitably, toward the conclusion of the beginning, everything seems neatly, grandly easy. There is that moment where audiences are inclined to relax and hope against hope that everything will work out fine.

Everything working out fine may be great in life, but on film it is unforgivably boring.

At that very last moment, where it appears events will proceed smoothly, an event occurs that blows all complacency sky-high. It may be as subtle as in *American Graffiti* when the Richard Dreyfuss character is merely smiled upon by the mystical girl in the phantom T-bird; he will search for her throughout the rest of the film and, indeed, the rest of his life. Or it may be as broad as the blood-soaked murder of future Godfather Corleone's mother before the boy's very eyes.

Invariably, beginnings end this way. All seems right and well and fit. Then, in a flash, all is wrong and nothing fits. And it is in the middle that the complications are played out.

Wrinkles and Reversals

If at the end of the Beginning a complication arises that launches the tale's fundamental conflict, throughout the Middle the plot thickens. And what thickens a plot are wrinkles and reversals, obstacles and complications.

Through the middle of *American Graffiti*, Richard Dreyfuss strides a perilous path strewn with impediments to his progress: gang members from another town try to do him in; he and his buddy experience a profound loss of faith, particularly as it relates to the pal's relationship with his girlfriend and the effect that has upon the relationship between the boys. He attempts futilely—or at least that's the way it seems—to reach the apparently unreachable disc jockey up at the radio station. All of these, of course, are obstacles—barriers tossed in the road before him. And they are also wrinkles where the plot twists, knots, turns upon itself.

Wrinkles, obstacles, impediments, complications are all clearly related to one another. Each interferes with the protagonist's forward motion, each requires him to take a step sideways, up, over, or even momentarily backward in order to arrive at that place where it was determined at the beginning of the tale he should go.

Because sometimes these related phenomena actually require a protagonist to retreat temporarily, it can be useful to consider them as reversals. In the skillfully wrought tale they foil the thrust, require diversion and a host of shaping devices. Regardless of how one designates them, by obstructing the straight and narrow path, they lend the tale dimension, which is a vital and elusive quality of story craft. The purely straight line is too direct to contain the desirable strangeness and fun that viewers rightly crave. A no-detours story compares unfavorably to the sculpted curves, whorls, burls, whirlpools, and abrasions created by a good writer's well-stocked arsenal of reversals.

Reversals also go a long way toward helping writers confront the twin-edged sword of predictability.

Predictability

Clearly, screen stories should not be too predictable; at the same time a certain dollop of predictability is to be desired.

How much predictability constitutes a dollop?

If this were an easily answered question, screenplays would be easy to write.

Obviously, audiences love surprises. And just as clearly, predictability can go a long way toward spoiling the excitement born of unexpected plot twists and turns. But if absolutely no predictability could be tolerated in a screenplay, we could watch every movie—even the finest—one time only. For once we know the way it comes out, that particular tale is totally and eternally predictable. Once we know "Rosebud" is the sled, we forever know "Rosebud" is the sled. Once we know that Jocasta is Oedipus's mother, can the revelation ever again surprise us?

And yet, like children, we love to hear the best-told tales endlessly repeated. And if in one or another retelling, just for variety, the tale is altered in even the tiniest facet, our listener rudely calls us back to the original text. If we view a print of *Psycho* and observe that *this* time Janet Leigh takes her shower, dries herself off, and climbs into bed for a good night's snooze, we will inspect the projector, the projectionist, our eyes, our medication to identify what in the world the trouble might be. Surprised as we should most surely be, we would feel also cheated.

While a smart writer has no desire to telegraph events before they occur, some predictability is nevertheless useful—even necessary—toward moving an audience through a tale.

If early in *Gremlins* we are told by the elderly Chinese shopkeeper that under no circumstances should the little critters come into contact with water, you can predict with certainty that they are going to be moistened before the last reel. Likewise, it is not for nothing that Shakespeare opens *Macbeth* with witches spelling out—albeit in riddles—precisely what is to occur within the tale. We can be damned certain Macbeth will be king, and that, somehow or other, Birnam Wood of Dunsinane will move.

A desirable predictability in movies compares effectively to the children's game of boo! What's more frightening? To walk down a corridor absolutely unaware that someone is going to jump out from behind a door, or *knowing* somebody is going to do just that?

On the surface it might seem the former is more unsettling, as the victim has no time to prepare. The truth, however, as everyone knows who has ever tried, is quite the opposite. Knowing someone is hiding behind that pillar or in that alcove or somewhere—anywhere—simply causes the victim to tighten, to tense, to flex every muscle in terrible anticipation of what is to come. And when it arrives, the effect is all the more shattering for its predictability.

When a script is criticized as predictable, what the critic truly means is that it is *too* predictable.

Coincidence

Screenplays are from time to time, with and without justification, accused also of being too coincidental.

Can a good writer include in his story a glaring, convenient coincidence? Yes—but only one will be tolerated per script.

Surely it has more than a little to do with the fact that life itself is riddled with coincidence. Indeed, an extraordinary coincidence in everyone's life—a special sperm conjoining with one particular egg—is the reason each of us is here.

But life is life and film is film; the former is free, the latter six bucks a pop. And for their money audiences rightly expect movies to be special and well worked out, the events skillfully orchestrated. A respectable movie tale may be launched or resolved by a coincidence. But beyond that people are entitled to see the story exquisitely crafted. They resent a dependence upon coincidence as they understand it for what it is: a writer's laziness.

If audiences will tolerate a single coincidence, screenwriters ought to make it important, make it launch the tale's fundamental action or appear later in the story for the resolution to rest upon.

Preston Sturges's *Christmas in July* is an example of the latter. Well-meaning friends deceive a pal into believing he has won a contest. In the end he actually *does* win. Why do audiences tolerate the coincidence? Partly because it's the only such coincidence in the tale.

In *The China Syndrome*, by perfectly acceptable coincidence, television reporter Jane Fonda, in the company of news cameraman Michael Douglas, just happens to be filming a story at a nuclear power plant at the precise moment that there occurs an "event" in which the reactor malfunctions.

Imagine if later in the picture, by some combination of twists and turns, the photographic footage of the event had been lost or destroyed. Imagine, also, that the news team responds by returning to the plant to shoot more footage. Imagine still further that they are deep in the midst of filming as *another* such event takes place.

Now imagine how audiences might react. They would be outraged, and rightly so. They would understand only too well that the reason the latest event occurs is because it happens to suit the writer's convenience.

But movie story structure—like movies themselves—is created to serve not the writer's but the audience's convenience.

Coincidences work best early in a tale, although they can usefully occur later. In either case, the significant principle is that wherever that coincidence is placed it must be the only coincidence in the entire script.

The Big Gloom

It is no coincidence, and also perfectly predictable, that by the end of the middle virtually every screenplay runs headlong into a formidable barrier. It is as if audiences by nature start fidgeting, stretching, yawning at this particular juncture. All too often this is exacerbated by the fact that scripts lacking shape tend to sprint from the very beginning. And like runners who fail to pace themselves, roughly four-fifths of the way through the tale screenplays also tend to lose their wind.

The baseball community addresses this problem with a well respected convention: the seventh-inning stretch.

You cannot stop a movie, however, an hour and twenty

minutes along, and invite everybody to stand and flex and kibitz for a few moments.

For the screenwriter another remedy is required.

Oddly, at this particular station, the writer needs to craft a low among lows, a deeply disturbing, horrible, dreadful moment when all appears forever and irretrievably lost. Naturally this cannot be some artificial appendage invented at the last moment; it must derive naturally from an already well-structured story.

If this grim moment—which by no means should be confused with the climax—occurs too early, at the conclusion of, say, the beginning, the entire script will run out of steam just at that point when the proper Big Gloom ought to descend.

In *American Graffiti* it is Dreyfuss's phone conversation with the phantom girl in the T-bird when he learns for once and for all that they will never, ever meet. This moment is darker and more frightening even than the flaming car wreck that soon follows and constitutes the climax. He realizes he will never find what he seeks, never truly fulfill his destiny, as long as he hangs around with his old buddies in his safe, stultifyingly familiar hometown.

In *Nothing in Common* it is the moment Tom Hanks comes to grips with the desperation of his father's medical condition. In *Terms of Endearment* it is the moment in the hospital when we learn of the impending demise of the young mother. In *About Last Night* it is the overly convenient montage in which a "liberated" Rob Lowe suffers miserably for his loss of commitment to the woman whom only a moment earlier he was so eager to shed.

The Big Gloom is that moment, occurring almost inevitably just before the beginning of the end, approximately eighty minutes into the film, where the protagonist is furthest from achieving his goal.

Endings

Place a white rat in a Skinner box—a cage with a trigger-controlled feed chute—and reward the charming fellow with a pellet of rat food not whenever he presses the lever but the first time he presses it after a particular interval in time.

With just a bit of experience the rat soon learns that pressing the lever does not always result in a reward; unsophisticated as one might imagine an albino rat to be, nevertheless he quickly gets the idea that he is rewarded only within some sort of time frame. A graph of lever-pressing reveals a flat, arbitrary number of pressings over a period, rising suddenly as the prearranged time interval approaches. Clearly, the rat "learns" that the end is in sight, and he presses frantically as the moment approaches.

Some will protest that it is not fair to compare humans and rats. But rats and humans share at least this single characteristic, which is pertinent to the art and the craft of screenwriting: When the end is in sight they sprint like crazy.

There is an old directors' and editors' trick for blocking and cutting love stories. When, after a long separation the lovers are finally reunited, they are seen first to gaze longingly at each other from opposite ends of the big screen. Then, slowly, each takes a step toward the other, and then another step, and another. And as the steps increase in number, so also does their pace. And finally, with the music swelling, the boy and the girl rush breathlessly toward each other in such a manner as to set a new Olympic record for the quarter-mile.

Writers also tend to sprint when the end of their screenplay appears at hand. However, it can be a serious mistake.

Ideally, of course, a script's conclusion is foretold in its opening. Once the tension is properly set, its resolution can be taken for granted, even if the required writing craft cannot. When the boys learn at the beginning of *Stand by Me* that there is a body in the woods, and that the bad guys, the older boys, also will be attempting to locate that body, we can accept as given that the young boys will find the body and that they will accomplish this feat before their antagonists.

This is so—this *has* to be so—because the purpose of endings is to resolve and balance beginnings and middles.

Natural as this process happens to be, it can be achieved only methodically, through the most painstaking deliberation. Scrambling madly just to get the pages finished is a recipe for disaster. Writers need to resist the urge to hurry as the conclusion of their script approaches.

Once the end arrives, and once it has fled, and once the final credits crawl across the screen and the curtains close and the house lights come up, the audience should feel not uplifted, not superior, not virtuous, but quite the contrary, humbled. To no small extent each viewer should be left with some sense of his status as one more wretched sinner. Each should be reminded of his own sweet and sour humanity. There should arise within each member a sense that what has transpired on the screen is really about him. There should resonate within the audience a sense that the situations depicted on screen obtain also for their own lives.

Ambiguity

Can a screen story be ambiguous?

Yes and no.

Art's worthy mission is not to achieve pat and pretty solutions to the existential problems dominating the intellect since the dawn of thought. Surely no mere movie can provide easy answers to questions that are by their nature unanswerable.

The purpose of creative expression is not to answer questions but to ask them. The worthy film refines and articulates important inquiries. Perhaps this explains why a film's end ought to be every bit as unsettling as it is settling. And while the burden is upon the writer to provide the audience a worthy tale populated by worthy characters, it is all right also to require the audience to work just a little.

A good example is found in *The Revolutionary* starring Jon Voight, a film made at the end of a lamentable late-sixties trend, when Hollywood attempted futilely and repeatedly to cash in on "revolution" as if it were the latest flavor of toothpaste. *The Revolutionary* went largely unnoticed, although it is arguably the single best movie in that sorry group. In the movie, Voight portrays a protagonist who is at first totally self-involved, uncommitted, unprincipled; through the body of the film he is rendered caring, moral, ethical. In the course of the film he must decide whether it is right or wrong to resort to violence in order to redress grievances. On one hand, isn't this precisely what George Washington and his merry band of guerrillas perpetrated in 1776? But on the other, won't innocent people be caused suffering and death?

Voight is confused. By film's end he arrives at something like a decision: He will hurl an incendiary device. But has he truly decided? Will he actually do it?

As the movie trods relentlessly toward its conclusion, his struggle is eloquently depicted. And just before that moment at which he is supposed to throw the bomb—or just before he does *not* throw the bomb—the image freezes and the film fades out. The final credits roll. The audience is asked, in effect, to provide its own solution to this philosophical quandary. Instead of providing an answer, they are invited to weigh the terrible, painful issues.

Another poignant example of a splendidly written film with a justifiably ambiguous ending is the screen adaptation of the first John LeCarré thriller, *The Spy Who Came In from the Cold*. Richard Burton plays a secret agent caught up in a richly convoluted plot involving spies, counterspies, counter-counterspies, and counter-counter counterspies. Double agents? Forget them; LeCarré provides triple, quadruple, quintuple agents. By film's end it is virtually impossible to determine who's on whose side. At the final fade Burton finds himself perched high atop the Berlin Wall with everybody shooting at him.

Whither shelter? On whose side will he ultimately settle?

Refusing to decide, the film leaves him lost in the netherworld of ambiguity.

It drives home the film's theme, which has nothing to do with right versus wrong or right versus left but, rather, with the nature of loyalty, and just as pertinent, the nature of disloyalty. The ambiguity, therefore, is integrated into the fabric of the entire film.

There is no question that ambiguity occupies a rightful place in movies, especially as it relates to their endings. As in all matters of creative expression, it is ultimately a question of balance.

Positive and Negative Space

The graphic-arts notion of positive and negative space can be useful to writers.

Simply stated, the positive space in, say, a portrait, is that area of the canvas occupied by the subject itself. The surrounding area—call it the background—represents the negative space.

Movie stories, even scenes within movies, also can be thought of as possessing both positive and negative space.

Consider the entire script by itself, from beginning to end, with all the characters, dialogue, and action between, as the positive space. It is everything occurring within the context of the film; it is everything actually viewed on screen.

But even before the beginning of a script there is implied backstory and filler. In every film we are properly given to believe that the characters and the tale do not spring full-blown from the first frame but that they lived before we met them. Similarly, once the film is over and the house lights go up, in the minds of both writer and audience the tale continues.

When *The Godfather, Part II* fades to its somber conclusion, with Michael alone, isolated from friends and family, staring off into space, we can imagine that his life nevertheless continues, however sorrowfully.

Likewise, the first images we see at the opening of *War-Games* involve military preparations to respond to a purported or simulated or actual nuclear attack—we don't know which. But we can be certain that there was life in these characters prior to these scenes, that the entire underground missile silo complex did not just arise in a flash but was there for some time. There is, in fact, no limit to the negative space's reach.

It is this limitlessness that differentiates negative from positive story space; the latter is finite and the former is not.

Some may consider negative and positive space as story versus plot, plot being that part of the story in the script, and story the boundless remains of the tale, forward and back.

The writer's task in confronting story craft is first to mark that precise point within the negative space where the positive commences. Call it the beginning. Similarly, seizing the precise moment to call it quits is to define the final boundary between positive and negative space. That point is, of course, the end.

Articulating the borders from one kind of space to another may appear a worthless task. But in fact it can be enormously useful in helping a writer determine precisely where the true beginning begins, i.e., that place before which nothing else is needed. In the same way it can help determine the end.

Again, creative expression consists of hard choices. Anything that facilitates those choices is to be welcomed.

Gravity—Cause and Effect

Stories move by a kind of gravity.

After Newton and until Einstein, gravity could be thought of as an invisible string tugging all objects toward the center of the earth. But after relativity, gravity became a more grandiose phenomenon. Instead of considering it somehow akin to an invisible string, it is useful to see it as an object's reluctance to remain wherever it happens to be.

Such tension pertains to stories. A well-crafted story does not want to rest; it wants desperately to keep moving.

Indeed, nowhere in nature is there anything like true stasis. Were an object somehow to succeed in making its way to the center of the earth, for example, it would not remain there. It would move with the earth itself, revolving on its axis, traveling in its orbit around the sun, flowing with the solar system and the galaxy through space.

All any object really "wants" is to travel to its next station on the space/time continuum. An object's "discomfort" at being forced temporarily to stand still is manifested in gravity.

However farfetched this all may appear, it is in fact broadly and practically useful for writers to view story this way. Something happens, and another event is caused to succeed it, and something else is compelled to follow; not just anything else but something that fits, something uniquely synchronous with the collected previous events. Thus a story moves forward. From time to time it may seem to rest, but rest is something it must in fact never do.

In *The Bedroom Window* illicit lovers witness a murder; they are required to concoct a fake explanation, which quickly comes to haunt them. In *A Great Wall* an executive is denied his richly earned promotion; the anger and disappointment prompt him to quit his job and stride off to the Far East in search of his roots. In *School Girl* a sociology student resolves to perform an objective, scholarly study of a particular social subculture; but it turns out to be the sexual subculture, and the protagonist's research techniques result in her becoming a convert to her subjects' cause.

Movies move. When even so successful a film as *Butch Cassidy and the Sundance Kid* abruptly halts its forward motion, requiring the audience to suffer smiling actors riding antique tricycles up and back across the screen to the accompaniment of "Raindrops Keep Falling on My Head," the tale grows cold. Writers must forever dodge the temptation to stand still, to regroup. Movie stories crank relentlessly forward at twenty-four frames per second. Like gravity, they grind ever onward, seeking resolution but never perfectly finding it.

Choices—Subtle and Unsubtle

Question: When should a film end?

Answer: (a) too soon; (b) too late; (c) at exactly the right moment.

If you chose (c) you are wrong. The correct answer is: (a) too soon. Clearly (b) too late is incorrect. For a film to drag on past that point after which nothing is needed is to squander an audience's attention.

But what about (c)?

The sorry truth is that human beings simply do not possess the capability to determine with authority "exactly the right moment," nor indeed, exactly the right anything, certainly not in matters of art.

By the process of elimination, therefore, the correct answer is (a) too soon. Another way to look at it is that too soon *is* exactly the right moment.

Perhaps this is merely a fancy way of reciting the old show-business cliche: Leave 'em wanting more. The audience ought to feel just a little disappointed, instead of relieved, that the film finally ends. This serves to propel the viewer past the ending into the implied negative space, the phantom tale existing *after* the tale.

The rule for beginnings and endings: Start late, finish early.

Theme—The So-What Test

Somewhere deep inside every worthy screen story, binding the characters, shaping the dialogue, integrating all the scenes lies a unifying thread succinctly answering the question: So what?

This is the movie's theme. After a film's final frame there

ought to be some clear sense of purpose, a reason for all the fuss and bother, a semblance of overall meaning.

It is no accident that this section on theme comes last among all those treating story. For among theme's most important characteristics is that it, too, follows story. A common destructive error committed by legions of inexperienced writers—and no small number of seasoned professionals—is first to fashion a theme and then to attempt to wrap a story around it. If ever there were a recipe for frustration in screenwriting it is precisely that, to place theme before tale, to let the tail wag the dog, to let ideas lead events instead of the other way around. To start with theme leads inevitably to art's lethal enemies: self-consciousness and heavy-handedness.

A student in an advanced screenwriting class at UCLA once suggested that while she wasn't yet sure what her story would be, she knew it would embrace a firm stance against pollution. I called for a show of hands in order to determine how many people in the class favored pollution.

There were no volunteers.

Of course it is commendable (if not exactly courageous) to oppose pollution. But the purpose of a script is not to take a stance on some issue, no matter how noble. A script's task is to tell a good story.

Story and theme do not exist independently. Each is a function of the other. Solid stories automatically contain themes. Story's nature is that beneath it lies a single operating principle, a basic premise: the theme.

Unwidely, preachy, theme-first scripts hustling issues with which everybody already agrees contribute nothing to film besides boredom. And to render pollution or any other crucial issue boring serves only to trivialize what ought to be a critical, arresting notion. In the end such writing serves only to support the very polluters the writer wishes to oppose.

Movies without themes sometimes offer fast, fleeting fun, but they do not stick to the ribs. *Outrageous Fortune* momentarily diverts us but soon fades from memory. *Tootsie* remains. The latter is about something; the former is not. The first is but a catalogue of zany antics; the second has something to say about an important human issue: gender.

If theme follows story, writers follow theme. This is simply to say that until his script is well under way the theme is largely invisible even to the writer. Sophocles struggling with *Oedipus Rex* could not have been trying to teach the world some timeless lesson about the nature of man and woman. Working writers of every generation must appreciate he was merely scrambling to get the pages finished by deadline.

That *Oedipus Rex* is what it is testifies only to its author's genius. He wasn't operating differently from other writers; he was merely superior.

Of course, we can only guess what Sophocles intended. But some modern writers are explicit about their story/ theme development. Arthur Miller, for example, volunteers that when he is approximately two-thirds of the way through a play its thematic substance suddenly becomes clear to him. He then writes the theme in a few brief words on an index card and pins it to the wall above his typewriter. That guides the rest of the writing, and illustrates what precisely it is within his play that is integrated and, as importantly, what is not. Most significant, however, is the simple fact that theme emerges later; before theme, before anything else, comes story.

There is an ancient Zen expression: You cannot hit a target by aiming at it. The expert archer feels his way toward the bull's-eye; it is more a product of the heart than any intellectual calculation. Similarly, good writers do not make important statements by trying to do so. Good writers write wonderful stories containing profound insights because that is story's nature.

Down on his luck behind a string of box office disasters, needing desperately to demonstrate he could make a profitable movie, Francis Coppola did his best work, *The Godfather*. Purchasing the rights to a best-selling, rough-and-tumble crime thriller, he created what has to be an authentic film classic. Later, when once again he wielded the power to do whatever he wanted, he made the "important" *One from the Heart*, which promptly vanished, as it so richly deserved.

Sometimes it seems there are but a handful of themes, which are treated over and over again by all kinds of writers in all kinds of ways. The adolescent coming-of-age motif is an example. Just because it is tackled successfully in, say, *American Graffiti* does not mean it can't be addressed again in a different but worthy fashion as in *My Bodyguard*, or *Stand by Me*, or *Lords of Flatbush*, or *Cooley High*, or *River's Edge, Over the Summer*, or any of a host of treatments.

The challenge, of course, is to attack the theme each time in a fresh way. But however skillful the writing, theme's nature is such that when it is spelled out in uncomplicated terms it appears trite, even silly. What, for example, is the theme of *Star Wars*? Good triumphs over evil; love is stronger than hate.

What is the theme of *E.T.*? Love thy neighbor. *E.T.* says that which is different, which frightens us, which appears ugly eventually may look rather cute and cuddly. It may nourish and sustain us, indeed, deliver us from evil. Surely writer Melissa Matheissen did not set out to say all that. Her assignment was simply to extend the tale of *Close Encounters of the Third Kind*, to build a story around the notion that the departing spacecraft leaves behind an alien child.

What is the theme of *Citizen Kane*? You can't buy love. A man who has everything—wealth, women, power—is nonetheless unhappy, friendless, loveless, unfulfilled.

Tootsie? Living as a woman makes a man a better man. *Kramer vs. Kramer*? Commitment is freedom; forging a bond with human beings is not limiting but expanding, not entrapping but liberating.

What is *The Godfather* all about? First, family. If on the surface it appears to be a tale of gangsters and crime, beneath lies a tale of brothers, the ways they get along, the ways they don't get along. And it is a tale of fate. Michael never intends to become the new don; it befalls him quite by chance.

Herein lies an important aspect of effectively articulated theme. The same threads weaving together the characters on the screen, no matter how foreign they appear compared to ourselves, somehow bind us also, cause to resonate in us something that affects our own lives, recapitulates our own experience, rings familiarly in our own struggle.

And what, as a final example, is the theme of *WarGames*? Antiwar? Pro-peace? Not in the least. *WarGames* simply preaches that human weakness is strength. More to the point, it suggests that frailty, our perfect imperfection, makes us not weak but strong, renders us not inferior but superior to all-perfect, unfeeling machines. The human link in the chain of command—foiling the nuclear attack—is presented not as a defect but as a special human strength. In *WarGames* it results in nothing less than the salvation of our species.

So what? *That's* what!

To reiterate, perhaps theme's single most important aspect is that it does not precede but instead follows story in screenwriting's developmental stages. And story itself begins not from ideas or concepts, but from incidents, actions, events. A writer observes something and for reasons he does not at first fully understand finds himself thinking about what he has seen. And if it haunts him for a sufficient period, he may find himself beginning to attach events to it that are wholly of his own creation. And, eventually out of all his ruminations he may begin to assemble some sort of shapely tale.

4

CHARACTER:

Only Human,

Humans Only

There are three basic rules for creating audience-worthy movie characters.

First: No stereotypes.

Second: Render everybody, even the foulest, most evil villain somehow sympathetic.

Third: Instead of having them lie there on a slab, static and stale, require your characters to grow and develop throughout the tale.

Let us examine the last item first.

Development

If many screenwriters grudgingly concede deficiencies in plot craft, they insist they know how to paint rich, broad, wacky, sensitive, insightful, touching, colorful characters.

They have merely to call upon memories of colorful characters they have known. Doesn't every family possess at least one dark sheep, invariably an uncle, who hasn't held a job since he got out of the navy? Does not every college dormitory hold a jokester who, underneath his clownish facade, is a deeply sensitive poet? Did not every writer once work as a waiter, or cabbie, or bartender, and meet a host of rich characters, each one of whom would provide a fabulous portrait for a movie?

These may seem on the surface to provide some promise for conflict, but in fact they are for the most part too familiar. And even in the best of circumstances, regardless of how arresting they may appear upon introduction, if screen characters remain exactly the same throughout a tale, if they do not change, grow, develop—or, at the very least if they are not *challenged* to do so—the audience will grow *for* them, and what the audience will grow is bored.

Characters who from the first minute on screen tell you everything there is to know about them are no different from real people who on first encounter regale you with every detail of their lives. Audiences are entitled to a bit of a tease, even a full-blown seduction, so that as a film matures new layers of identity are stripped away, resulting in continually burgeoning intrigue.

Truly memorable screen characters start somewhere and end up somewhere else.

Dustin Hoffman in *Kramer vs. Kramer* starts out selfish, insensitive, narcissistic; he ends up expanded, connected, fulfilled.

Midnight Cowboy's Ratso, another Hoffman portrayal, is introduced as a thieving, lying, rancid, scuzzy maggot; he finishes the film caring, considerate, and honest, if also dead.

Michael Corleone at the start of *The Godfather* is innocent, moral, principled; by tale's end he's bereaved, bereft, heartless, soulless, a power-mongering murderer of, among countless other victims, his own brother.

Ralph Kramden at the opening of every *Honeymooners* episode is obstinate, inflated, blustery, pigheaded, wrongheaded; by the final fade he invariably is contrite, humble, patient, affectionate.

It's hard enough to create a character who, even at first glance, is special enough to merit an audience's attention. But once that is accomplished the real work remains. And that work consists of expanding and enhancing the character's humanity throughout the film.

Must a character change?

Not necessarily. Patton is still Patton at the end of *Patton*— every bit the possessed warrior he always was. But in the course of the movie his character has been challenged, articulated and rearticulated in such a manner as to provide a glimpse into why he is who he is. And even if we don't exactly like him, we are fascinated. Passing two hours with him in a movie theater proves a worthy expenditure of our time.

Sympathy

Complicated characters, rounded and whole, are infinitely more fun than folks whose entire book can be read in a single superficial flash. And nothing renders characters— even lying, scheming, conniving frends—fleshy and full like a pinch of sympathetic human understanding.

Sympathy for one's characters raises a tale above the mindless equation in which everything fits perfectly but is also quite perfectly dull.

Years ago, to seize a brief respite from the summer's paralyzing heat, my parents took me to my first film, the Disney live action classic *Treasure Island*. There is no forgetting, in particular, Robert Newton's performance as the antagonist, crusty old peg-legged Long John Silver, a scoundrel among scoundrels. He torments young Jim Hawkins— Newton deliciously pronounces it " 'Arkins"—separates him from his beloved comrades, holds him hostage, threatens his life, renders his frail subsistence just generally miserable until, at last, on the beach, at film's end, the British sailors close in upon him, certain to liberate the youngster and deliver Silver to the law.

At the shore, the waves licking at his one good foot, Long John struggles futilely to free the lonely little skiff from the slippery sand in which it is mired. In all of God's creation was there ever a more pathetic, desperate figure than Silver at this moment? No human could fail to pity him. His wooden leg repeatedly slips in the sand, making it impossible for him to launch the dinghy. The wicked old buccaneer resembles an overturned turtle struggling pathetically to right itself.

But at the last moment, with the British troops now sprinting into view on the ribbon of beach at jungle's edge, young 'Arkins unexpectedly leaps into action, surprising even himself. Urgently he collaborates with his oppressor, setting his shoulder against the vessel's gunwale, joining forces with Silver in a final, desperate attempt to save the old curmudgeon.

And as the boat now slips past the breakers, carrying the pirate beyond the reach of his pursuers, we share both Hawkins's and Silver's pleasure at the escape. Despite his bloody record and evil heart, there is some shred of humanity in him; we rejoice in his redemption.

Perhaps it provides us just a glimmer of hope for our own undeserved salvation.

J. R. Ewing of television's *Dallas* is an unreconstructed scum-hook who is still somehow deeply sympathetic. J. R. lies and cheats his reckless way to the top of the Texas oil world. He is faithless to his wife, to his friends, to his business associates, to his own brother and sister. In one episode, through a shady deal involving the illegal export of fuel to Cuba, he even betrays his country.

Nevertheless, through it all there is something unavoidably likable about the guy. His fragile, false smile and nervous, calculated twinkle endear him to us. Beneath all the synthetic good-old-boy bluster, we see nobody other than a lonely, left-out little lad trying to win his daddy's attention and approval. (This continues to be the case even though—in the series' later seasons—Daddy is long dead.)

Do not all real-life human relationships transcend even the physical presence of the principals long after they are gone? Who among us in our hearts does not mourn daily the failed gesture, the lost courtesy we might once have offered a friend or sibling or parent who is now removed forever from our proximity? Who can say with serene confidence he was won the unconditional validation of his mother and father?

When J. R. misbehaves, therefore, we see nothing but the naughty little boy with his hand in the cookie jar, hoping yet again for that reassuring, affectionate nod from his long-lost daddy.

Instead of wanting to knock him to the ground and grind his face beneath our heel, we are moved to cuddle and comfort, to stroke and protect the wounded, trembling little fawn. His heartache is our own. There resonates within us something of our own humanity, our own pain, our disappointment and shortcomings.

Such rich characterizations have been with us since the dawn of dramatic writing.

Oedipus kills his father. Next, he violates the ultimate taboo—incest. Our hero, the king, lustily and repeatedly engages in sexual intercourse with his mother. Consider the lengths to which Sophocles goes to maintain the audience's sympathy for such a character, fully appreciating that without such sympathy there is no play but merely, at best, a darkly evil sketch.

First and foremost, as already addressed in Chapter 3, he constructs a plot that protects Oedipus from knowledge of the true facts of his coupling; who could forgive a protagonist who *knowingly* copulates with his mother? Further, upon learning the sorry truth of his situation. Oedipus is genuinely regretful.

Through these devices the writer enables us to experience fondness for our hero despite the unspeakable acts he perpetrates. The ancient Greek master appreciates how important it is for every member of the audience to cherish the time spent with the entire population of his play, no matter how heinous any particular character's crime may be.

Television's Archie Bunker is yet another ready example. Archie is a bigot and, like most bigots, not especially bright. But who among us possesses positively no trace of prejudice? Archie may be stubborn beyond reason, blind to his own emotional and intellectual handicaps, but he is also unmistakably human. We learn to love the bigot at the same time as we revile the bigotry.

Our exposure to Archie makes us that much more capable of examining our own biases. We are perhaps a tad less judgmental of others. Our capacity for toleration is expanded.

Another useful illustration of sympathy's critical role is found in a comparison between two films—*Z* and *The Battle of Algiers*. The former is the more widely known but, in my view, the inferior of the two. The problem lies primarily with the treatment of villains, in this case the plundering, antidemocratic Greek generals who stage the military coup that will imprison their land for more than a decade. In *Z* they are depicted as buffoons, fools without a shred of humanity. Remember, in real life it may be true that they were precisely this way; nevertheless, here we are concerned not with historical accuracy but superior drama.

Such treatment reduces *Z* to shallow good-guys-versus-bad-guys; hiss the black hats, cheer the white hats. And whatever tension and excitement is created by skillful cinematography, editing, and a pounding musical score is mitigated by characters who appear contrived.

In *The Battle of Algiers*, however, even as the writer pulls no punches regarding the side he favors (the Algerian independence fighters), the enemy (the imperial French establishment and, especially, its military governors) is treated with a cautious but palpable dignity. That the bad guys are not born evil, are not naturally bent on destruction, makes them no less horrifying but, quite the contrary, all the more so. They are, like all of us, the product of their heritage, the collective beliefs and biases unavoidably imparted to them by the culture in which they are reared.

Miraculously, instead of excusing the French generals, instead of expiating their guilt, this evenhanded treatment renders them all the more culpable.

It requires us to consider all sides, to experience the pain attendant on hard moral choices. The native-born Algerian terrorists, although they are clearly the heroes in this piece, are depicted also as the murderers of innocent children. The French militarists, similarly, even as they are unabashedly antagonistic, are seen clinging to what they view as the safe and sane social order.

The Japanese commander of the jungle prison camp in *The Bridge on the River Kwai* is one more example of an unrepentant tyrant whose humanity is nevertheless permitted to show, vastly enhancing not only the characterization but the entire film. He violates the international laws pertaining to prisoners of war. Ruthlessly he locks his wards in hot boxes, humiliates and tortures them. Yet the Carl Foreman-Michael Wilson screenplay allows the audience to see him also as one more unfortunate wretch just doing his sorry, dreadful job. We are even permitted to see him weep.

It is a far stronger, more memorable portrait than the run-of the-mill bad guy.

Clearly, fine films abound with potentially unredeemable figures redeemed. Probably the best example of all appears early in *The Grapes of Wrath* when a bulldozer arrives, a growling, fire-breathing metal dragon, to raze the neighbors' farm where the Joads have stayed since losing their own spread. The farmer stands firm, shotgun at the ready, announcing to the machine's operator that he's ready to commit murder in order to save his home. The driver, his eyes concealed behind goggles, his nose and mouth wrapped in a bandana to ward off the dust, appears very much like an alien from Jupiter. But when he temporarily brakes the bulldozer, lifts the goggles, and raises the bandana, we recognize that this is but another neighbor, who's lost *his* farm, and whose wretched fortune is to have won this job working for the bank, running over his neighbors' farms. That he is in fact no monster but just another human, indeed, a dear old friend, makes his task that much sadder, and the audience's emotion that much more palpable.

Human treatment of human characters inevitably provides for heightened drama, a goal screenwriters ought consummately to desire.

Stereotypes

Mainstream filmmaking suffers from a plague of type-casting. And this pertains not exclusively to actors but to virtually all other film artists, including writers.

A writer, if he's lucky enough to become known at all, likely becomes known as a comedy writer or an action/adventure writer, a melodrama writer, a woman's writer, a man's writer. Sadly, writers themselves frequently contribute to this obsession by populating their scripts with hordes of ready-made, all too familiar characterizations, more caricature than character.

There are in fact just two kinds of writers: good writers and bad writers. And good writers avoid types altogether in their scripts.

It is so much easier to jam a type into a script—the hard-hearted businessman, the good-hearted Irish priest, the beer-swilling hard hat, the by-the-books cop, the dumb blonde—than to create a fresh, original character whom audiences will remember for his uniqueness, the differences instead of the similarities, the special qualities that render him not like but unlike everybody else.

Overall there are two reasons to avoid types.

First of all, the generalizing that creates types is precisely the operating principle behind bigotry. Ivan Boesky steals and plunders his way through Wall Street? *All* Jews are swindlers. Idi Amin spreads death and destruction across his land? *All* blacks are incapable of providing enlightened, democratic leadership. An Arab murders innocent civilians in a terrorist bombing at an airport? *All* Arabs are crazed killers, eager to wreck the lives of women and children.

Such thinking not only poisons the human spirit; it also makes for rotten movies. If writers of public and popular art don't battle to consign bigotry to its rightful rest, who shall assume the task? Certainly screenwriters have no stake in perpetuating racial, ethnic, sexist, or cultural typing.

But there is an even better reason to avoid writing such types—*any* types—into movies. They're boring.

How could they be anything else?

The reason weak, inexperienced writers include types instead of characters in their scripts is also the reason to avoid them. For in movies as in life, characters we immediately recognize because we've seen them before are neither interesting nor memorable. Folks who upon first glance are already known to us are not worth getting to know.

People in films ought to be fun to watch. How does a writer invent such characters? First, by making them different from—not similar to—everybody else we see in movie after movie. A useful technique is simply to imagine the most familiar stereotype and then present its exact opposite.

Consider the late-sixties Oscar-winner *In the Heat of the Night*. Screenwriter Sterling Silliphant's portrait of a backward, backwoods redneck sheriff is first-rate writing, but the character spawned countless imitations. Today it would be grand fun to depict a rural southern sheriff who is a faithful and devoted servant of justice, brimming with dignity and intelligence, imbued with an abiding reverence for truth.

The square peg in the round hole is so much more fun than that which fits neatly, familiarly.

A nun, devoted to God as she may well be but who happens also to be a baseball fanatic, a walking encyclopedia of standings and statistics, is different from what we have seen and should prove good fun to watch on screen.

A big-city police lieutenant who happens to be a closet medievalist, who has studied eighth-century literature, who is an expert on Carolingian history, offers audiences a welcome diversion from the four trillion hard-bitten cop clones we see again and again in too many movies and television shows.

A down-and-dirty street-wise ghetto youth who quietly and secretly accumulates a world-class stamp collection and thereby an uncanny knowledge of history, geography, and a circumspect world view, sure beats the ten-zillionth shoplifting/knife-wielding baddest-assed dude this wrongside of the tracks.

As long as the writer struggles to keep it credible, there is almost no limit to the ways in which he can invigorate a script with fascinating, unpredictable characters.

In a recent screenplay by a student at UCLA, a mother is outraged because her young son is inadvertently exposed to pornography. The boy's father attempts to calm his wife, to reassure her that it's no big deal, that she's making far too much of the whole thing, that sooner or later the kid has to find out about these things and there's no true cause for alarm.

But isn't it more fun if it's the *father* who's all hot and bothered over the kid's having seen some dirty photos and the *mother* who reassures the father and belittles his concern?

Isn't it men, after all, who are actually more prudish, more Victorian in their attitudes about sex? And in Western society, if the truth be told, isn't it women who handle this sensitive subject with the greater sophistication?

Some years ago, with a major convention coming to the city, a New York reporter overheard some cabdrivers gloating over the prospect of having swarms of out-of-towners about, ripe pickings for their crooked ways. The reporter set out to do an exposé of thieving cab drivers. Dressed in a European-cut suit, affecting a fraudulent European accent, carrying foreign currency, he attempted to entice taxi operators into cheating him. He set himself up as the perfect pigeon, virtually pleading with cabbies to take advantage of him—but he could not entice a single driver to cheat him!

It's one more monument to the wrongheadedness of generalizing about *any* group—even New York City taxi drivers. In real life it makes for poor human relations and in movies it makes for uninteresting characters.

Avoid, lose, and eschew types.

Turn them upside down.

Keep Character Descriptions Brief

Ideally, characters should be introduced to a screenplay's readers exactly as they are to be revealed to the audience viewing the film on screen. The proper place, therefore, to describe characters is where they first appear within the script. And these descriptions, along with everything else in a screenplay, should be brief and to the point.

There are basically only two points of information to establish at the outset: gender and age.

Long, convoluted descriptions of a character's peculiar physical attributes, his past, his pets, the car he drives (even though he doesn't drive a car in this picture), the musical instrument he would play if he played a musical instrument, are to be avoided. It would be bad enough if such descriptions were merely useless. In fact, they are worse than useless, as they make for a harder read. And they betray the writer's inexperience, his unfamiliarity with the form.

It is much easier to describe a character's rich, broad traits than it is actually to *create* such a character through action and dialogue.

Specifications, therefore, as to weight, height, coloring—if they are not integrated directly into the tale—serve only to restrict both character and casting. Don't say the hero is a redhead unless it is required by some specific story point that he be a redhead. Don't specify that the antagonist is extremely fat unless it is somehow a part of the story that he be fat. The producer and director will either obey the writer (highly unlikely) and eliminate a perfectly good actor who happens to be thin, or, more likely, they will recognize that the writer knows precious little about screenwriting and ignore him altogether.

Characters' physical and emotional traits ought to grow from what they say and do. Their actions and dialogue define them. What they do and say *is* their character.

Use Sensible Names

An expectant mother was recently overheard discussing names under consideration for her soon-to-be-born child. Robin, Pat, Kelly, Terry, Ronnie, and Bobby were among them. The mother explained that this enabled her to avoid the problem of having separate sets of names—one for girls and another for boys.

The very reason that may be sensible for an expectant mother is why it is senseless for screenwriters.

On screen an audience will immediately recognize a character's gender and age from its appearance; on the page, however, the description alone serves this purpose.

Names can be useful in this regard.

No reader will doubt the gender of a Mary or an Elizabeth, a Martin or a Fred.

And it makes good sense also to avoid assigning characters names that sound even the least bit alike—it makes for unnecessary confusion. Don't have a character named Harry and another named Larry. Avoid characters whose names have even the same initial—if you've got a Linda in your script why in the world would you also include a Lisa? The only exception should be in the case of some integrated plot point—for example, people with the same initials whose luggage gets mixed up with due consequences.

Invent

Don't describe all your women as beautiful and all your men as handsome. Language is the writer's stock in trade, and he ought to exploit it. If a screenwriter is properly economical in his descriptions, there is room to add just that little taste of insight that brings a character into relief. There is sufficient space to provide that extra giggle to coax readers to want to know more about him.

Real characters and reel characters are different from

one another in so many ways, but, first and last, both are reflections of flesh-and-blood man and mankind. And if it is true, as Aristotle asserts, that not character but story is the first principle of solid dramatic craft, it is a film's characters who remain vivid long after the story grows fuzzy in viewers' recollections.

Charles Foster Kane stays with us even as the specific twists and turns of *Citizen Kane* become enfolded in time's obscurity. Don Corleone is with us always and above all other characters in *The Godfather* even though he occupies a relatively abbreviated portion of that grand film. J. R. Ewing's precise shenanigans become lost in the fog of too many seasons, but J. R. himself is forever sharply etched into our minds.

Screenwriters need to let every character be human, to let the best and the worst of them challenge something within us to resonate with sympathy. Their sweet sorrow must touch our hearts. Their joy should recall our own. Writers should see to it that their characters' imperfections cause us to celebrate and expand our human tolerance.

5

DIALOGUE:

Talk Is Cheap

Years ago, sometime during the middle 1950s, flamboyant film producer Mike Tood introduced an artistic and technological innovation that for several minutes promised to change the entire face—or at least the nose—of motion pictures. It was designated, perhaps more appropriately than intended, Smell-O-Vision.

A tale, perhaps apocryphal, is told of its public debut.

The first—and final—movie utilizing this process opened with a scene in an evergreen Sierra setting. Simultaneously, atomized Pine Sol was sprayed into the auditorium. There soon rode across the screen a lone cowboy who set up camp and lit a crackling fire. On cue, an aroma of smoldering mesquite chips was released through the theater's air-conditioning ducts.

Tragically, this latter effect promptly ran amok. The theater filled with smoke, there arose among the audience a chorus of vigorous coughing. Obscured by thickening haze, the image on screen grew dim. In the lobby, a customer stocking up on Jujubes at the candy counter caught a whiff of the fumes and yanked the fire alarm. Projection was halted and the hall cleared of patrons and smoke.

Had Smell-O-Vision come to enjoy the success of earlier technical advances—sound, for example—screenwriters today would worry about three basic details in their scripts: sight, sound, and smell.

Instead they need concern themselves exclusively with two.

For if screenplays are in essence elaborate catalogues of details—character, plot, dialogue, action, setting, and others—it is easy to forget that all this information is conveyed solely via two distinct classes of data: what you hear and what you see. What's more, the emphasis falls heavily upon the former.

This may well appear to be a contradiction. At any given cocktail party, when profound insights run dry after the first quarter hour, and with everybody in the universe an expert on movies, inevitably someone pronounces the weary cliche that film is a visual medium.

And indeed: Moving pictures are first and foremost *pictures*.

Consider that when I was a film student at the University of Southern California in the late sixties, sound movies, films with synchronized audible tracks wedded to the image, had finally come to exist for a period merely equal to that of silents.

Silent film writers required no extraordinary insight to appreciate that audiences were not in the theater to read endless series of projected cards smeared with speeches, no matter how elegant the calligraphy. Like today's audiences, they demanded physical, visual, dramatic action.

Still, there is no getting around the fact that a good movie script is mainly talk.

This is not to suggest that there isn't a monumental difference between a talking and a talky picture. But the fact remains: Open a modern screenplay and you're looking mainly at dialogue.

Given the notoriously feeble attention span belonging to too many readers, visual detail in a script—character and scene descriptions, pieces of dramatic action—is commonly referred to as "all that black stuff," because on the page it appears to be just that, random smatterings of ink grouped into bulky rectangular blocks separating the dialogue.

Painful to relate, a large number of producers and agents read only dialogue. If the writer is lucky, or expensive, the visual descriptions might be lightly skimmed. Here is ample cause for screenwriters to weave dialogue that is special, sparkling, pleasurable, painful, punchy, poetic, every word worthy, every line crackling. And it never hurts to be funny.

Each speech, however brief, must be worth hearing. Along with every other aspect of screenwriting, dialogue must perpetually expand our knowledge of the characters at the same time as it advances the tale.

It's one more reason to keep scripts lean, neat, spare, devoid of detail and dialogue that is not absolutely essential. Movies projected onto the screen are, of course, fairly fecund with detail, but with precious exceptions these are photographed, not written. In a single frame's flash the camera tells more of a kiss or a sunset than the cumulative wordage of all the writers who have ever written.

But do not movie sound tracks contain components besides dialogue?

Yes.

How many such components?

Two.

What are they?

Music and effects.

What advice can we offer the screenwriter relative to music and sound effects in his script?

Leave them out!

There are, of course, exceptions. The test is always the same: integration. Is the music or effect linked to other aspects of the script? Is it necessary to the tale? Does it advance the plot? Does it move the characters?

Consider the true story of a celebrated film music composer. In his hungrier days, he lived in the Echo Park section of Los Angeles, a sparsely settled hilly area that for a gruesome time happened to serve as the drop-off point for victims of the Hollywood Strangler, a Glendale auto upholsterer whose hobby was murdering prostitutes and hitchhikers. Like so many musicians, our film scorer worked only at night, because only at night is there sufficient silence to summon the tranquil Zen oneness so vital to composing jingles for underarm deodorant spray.

On such a night, in the detached garage he had converted into a small music studio, he toiled to construct a musical motif appropriate to enhancing televised images of a client's brand of floor wax.

Jammed among his keyboards and synthesizers, his half dozen dogs asleep at his feet, he slowly wrote and rewrote an arresting, original, irresistible six-note figure. He played the figure and played it again, adjusting it here, there, readjusting until, after eight hundred tries, he had it nearly half right.

Suddenly the dogs went crazy. Collectively their eyes popped open, their heads jerked high, and they commenced an unsolicited chorus of angry, agitated yapping.

Their master himself now came alive, scolding the pups, cajoling, now imploring them to silence. Still they would not quit.

Over their din the composer now made out other sounds—a car door slam, footsteps in the thicket, snapping twigs, rustling dry grass, a swishing of branches. Soon enough the car door slammed once more. This was immediately followed by the high-pitched yip of tires turning too quickly, and the obligatory roar of an automobile engine.

Finally, silence was restored. The dogs settled back into their snooze.

Near dawn, his assignment at last concluded, the composer himself sank into deep slumber exactly where he sat. He was awakened two hours later by the sound of sirens, helicopters, and policemen rapping at his door. They were full of questions. Had he been here all night? Had he heard anything unusual?

He related the disturbance involving the dogs, the car, the sounds in the bushes. Why, he inquired, were they asking?

Because the Hollywood Strangler had dropped off a body not ten yards away midst the tall grass and tangled shrubs on the vacant hillside across the street. As part of their investigation, the police were eager to pinpoint the hour.

That's the end of the true story.

It's not exactly Academy Award time, but it offers pertinent examples of plot-advancing sound effects—car doors, tires, engine, snapping twigs, rustling bushes—all of which would be wholly appropriate to include in such a screenplay because they are integrated into the tale.

Let us now take the tale another step; let's invent.

The police depart and the composer retires to his bed. He rises at two and drives into Hollywood to drop off last night's charts with his copyist. By now it's three in the afternoon, a reasonable hour for a musician's breakfast. He enters a forbidding greasy spoon on a decrepit side street. He peacefully guzzles coffee, leafs through the recording industry trade rags, and hardly notices the shop's only other customer down at the far end of the counter, a lanky, scrawny, wasted middle-aged guy smoking a cigarette and reading the newspaper's account of the latest strangling.

Unconsciously, the stranger puckers his lips to whistle. The melody that emerges is arresting, original, irresistible. It's a mere tune, a simple little six-note ditty, but to the composer it is eerie, chilling, frightening, horrifying beyond measure. Worst of all, it is uncannily familiar. It stops him cold, sends shivers up his spine, and at the same time causes his sweat glands to seep full bore.

It's the jingle he wrote last night!

Who beyond our composer could know this tune? Can the fellow at the end of the counter be anybody but the Strangler?

If that's a responsible wrinkle for a story, we can once again thank integration. One event is connected to another. Note, also, that the invented portion of the tale is much more fun than the actual facts. Here is one more example of the necessity to avoid truth if you want to be a good movie writer.

But the primary reason we tell this fragment of a tale is because it offers a rare example of music meriting mention in a script. If the music in your script is as inextricably bound up in character and story, by all means describe it in the wide margins—the "black stuff"—of your script.

Otherwise leave it out.

But what about background music?

At the opening of Lawrence Kasdan's *The Big Chill,* the principal players are seen in various locations packing their respective bags for a journey. In the background plays Marvin Gaye's version of "I Heard It Through the Grapevine." Perhaps the writer utilized the music to set the period. The recording was, after all, popular during the characters' college days. But like so many golden oldies, it's probably playing at this very minute on forty random radio stations across America. Its ability to clue the audience as to period is, therefore, imperfect.

But beyond period, it can be argued the featured players have all learned "through the grapevine" of their mutual pal's suicide, the picture's catalyzing plot thrust.

Is it appropriate for the writer to specify the tune in the script? Unequivocally and without hesitation, the answer is: perhaps. In fact the question can be answered only with another question: Is it integrated? What is certain is that you cannot whimsically toss tunes into screenplays simply because you develop a moment's hankering for a taste of Marvin Gaye.

In sum, relative to music and sound effects, the screenwriter needs to discriminate regarding such details.

In movies, as in life, actions speak louder—and more eloquently, more articulately—than words. Accordingly, screenwriters should favor the visual over the conversational. The last thing an audience wants is to have characters lecture them.

Still, as we've noted, film scripts are mainly dialogue.

Quite some years ago, well into the sound era, a picture called *The Thief* was made without a single word of dialogue. For all the writer's courageous experimentation, the movie ended up awkward, confusing, and self-conscious. Predictably, the experiment succeeded merely in demonstrating how vital dialogue truly is.

Since screenwriters are stuck with dialogue, it is appropriate to consider common tricks and traps.

Avoid Reality

The grittiest, most naturalistic, most hard-bitten movie is nevertheless fantasy. The writer's charge is to present not reality but a thoroughly credible facsimile of reality.

Inexperienced writers commonly create dialogue replete with y'know, ummm, errr, hey, look, listen, I think, by the way, and a host of other hedges and thrust-blunting interjections. Challenged, the new writer typically responds: "That's the way people really talk."

But the way people really talk is for free; the way people talk in movies costs six dollars.

The way people really talk is to bob and weave, to wander, meander, tack, equivocate, beat around the bush. The way people really talk is to pass time. But in movies the way people talk must be pointed, purposeful. Each and every line must carry story and character freight.

The astute screenwriter provides only the full, spelled-out English words and allows the actors to hem, haw, and hesitate as appropriate to the drama inherent in the scene and situation.

Economize

Creative economy challenges all artists to say lots with little, not the other way around. Every line needs a clear purpose. Screenwriters are not paid by the word.

Ideally, dialogue must in a single stroke accomplish two goals—expand characters and advance plot. In *Escape from Alcatraz,* a prison psychologist inquires of the protagonist, portrayed by Clint Eastwood, "What was your childhood like?"

Eastwood's reply: "Short."

With a single word he tells us more of his hard-knocks upbringing, his deprived, disadvantaged, loveless roots, than thousands of pages of speeches on rough times, this crazy, cockeyed world, the grim and gritty neighborhood where he was raised, the mean kids who used to beat him daily, the cynical teachers who humiliated and abused him, his wicked dope-dealing stepmother, his absent father, his cute, fluffy, floppy-eared little puppy who got run over.

Of every bit of dialogue the writer must ask himself: Does this line move the tale? Does it tell us something new about the characters? And even if it does, is there a faster, fresher, more efficient, more economical way to accomplish the purpose?

No Repeats

Unless it is for emphasis or irony, or an attempt to hook or link lines so that they flow more rhythmically, don't have characters tell us what they already told us. Far from underscoring the point or purpose, this blunts the film's thrust.

In the film *Yentl*, there is a written prologue informing us that in olden Eastern Europe education was available only to men. The handful of women who managed to achieve literacy were restricted to reading superficial romances. Scholarly works were for men alone.

Just to be certain nobody in the audience misses the point, no sooner does the prologue fade than a bookseller rides his cart across the screen hollering, "Books for sale! Scholarly books for men! Romantic novels for women!" If that's not enough, he repeats it at least a dozen times.

Soon, Yentl makes her way to town, where the bookseller has set up shop. She sneaks over to his cart and begins to peruse a scholarly tome. The bookseller catches her, seizes the book, and reminds both Yentl and the audience yet again—perhaps they forgot in the half minute that has elapsed since they were last informed—that scholarly books are exclusively for men and that she, a woman, is limited to frivolous, superficial tales of romantic love.

The audience may not be consciously aware, but subliminally they must surely sense they are being taken for imbeciles. In this covert testimony to the writer's disdain for them, an otherwise courageous, splendid film distances itself from its viewers.

Writers may repeat only if it's not repetitive.

Consider, for example, the classic Japanese film *Rashomon*. Four observers tell the same story four times. Yet each participant's version is somehow unique, and the effect is to enhance our own vantage on the tale. Eventually a profound lesson emerges involving nothing less than the nature of human perception and truth itself.

No Chitchat

Life is positively rancid with prattle.

Hi, how are you? — Fine, thanks. Yourself? — Not bad, thanks. — The family? — Just great, though the baby has a rash. You? — Excellent. Say, would you like a cup of coffee? — Sounds great. — How do you take it? Sugar? Cream? Milk? Low fat? Skim? — Black, thanks. Have you any Sweet 'N' Low? — No, but I have Nutrasweet. — This is some beautiful day, isn't it? — Sure is, but they said on the radio that it might rain.

This is the kind of dialogue that, when contained in a film, causes audiences to storm the booth and hang the projectionist with a celluloid noose. It may be natural, but it's certainly not economical, does not advance the plot or expand our appreciation of the characters, and ought to be banished from screenplays.

Bad movies and television are, of course, riddled with such trifling talk. One can only attribute its abundance to writers' laziness. It is, after all, far easier to spin time-passing, page-adding blather than to craft succinct, pointed, purposeful, confrontational language that excites and moves an assembled mass of people.

Chitchat has a place only when it expands beyond its own immediate realm and attaches itself thematically to a film's central thrust.

In Reginald Rose's *12 Angry Men,* for example, at the conclusion of the trial, on the steps outside the courthouse, one of the jurors says to another: "I never caught your name." The two exchange standard introductions, then shrug, bid casual good-byes, and go their separate ways.

But here the apparent chitchat carries a serious and deeply probing subtext. The tale is an homage to the miracle of American jurisprudence whereby common, everyday folk gather together in jury rooms for no lesser purpose than the pursuit of justice and truth. That this noble undertaking is accomplished by total strangers ignorant even of each others' names is underscored by that modest and proper pinch of chitchat at story's end.

British playwright/screenwriter Harold Pinter often embraces, with uneven success, seemingly inconsequential small talk in a way that mirrors the subsurface battles raging among us all. In his movies and plays, the typical chitchat around the breakfast table becomes a metaphor for the despair of people too close to each other for too many years. The polite, seemingly cheery verbal jousting replaces authentic human interaction.

If a writer wishes to utilize chitchat in this manner he'd better be brilliant like Pinter. And as noted, even Pinter frequently overreaches and falls on his face.

A charming adolescent coming-of-age screenplay written by a student at UCLA was in its earliest draft saturated with polite, impact-squandering courtesies, pointless greetings, salutations. Virtually every scene started with choruses of "Hi, Debbie," answered with "Hi, Tom," and "Hi, Pete," and "Hi, Holly," and on and on before any scene ever truly got started, before any authentic drama was genuinely joined.

If the no-freight greetings were removed, the entire script would shrink by twenty pages. Confronted with the chit-chat's blemish, the writer responded, "Yeah, but that's the way teens talk, it's the way they measure each other, it's the way they chart their personal and emotional territory."

Nevertheless, just before completing the final draft, the writer decided to attempt to find some alternative language. At one particular scene's opening, instead of "Hi, Debbie," "Hi, Tom," he had Tom lead off with "Sexy dress!"

Debbie's response: "Like it?"

Tom: "*Love* it!"

Granted, this is not poetry rivaling Shakespeare, but surely it beats an endless tattoo of Hi-Debbie-Hi-Tom-Hi-Marci-Hi-Ted. It is quietly provocative, erotic, a much better measuring among adolescents than any chitchatty exchange of limp, listless greetings.

Liberated from chitchat, the writer returned to the script's beginning, located each "Hi" opening, and sharpened the entire screenplay. This resulted in a far more affecting, dramatic script.

Get to the Point

In the chapter on story structure, I said that inexperienced writers typically start their tale before its natural beginning. They make the same mistake with dialogue.

It's like watching TV on a slow news day when, in one of those pointless man-in-the-street interviews, a reporter encounters some hapless soul waiting on line for a bus and posits a profoundly probing query on the order of: "What do you think about taxes?"

Invariably Joe Citizen responds: "Taxes? Me? You want to know what I think? About taxes? Me? Taxes? Well, since you asked, I'll tell you. If you're seriously interested in knowing what I really, truly think about taxes, believe me, I'm happy to relate it to you since you have, after all, inquired. Now, remember, this is just my opinion, I'm speaking just for myself, not for the next guy, not for my wife, not for my church, not for my dog, not for my kid, not for anybody besides myself. You really want to know? Do you? Okay, I'll tell you. Frankly stated, to put it candidly, to say it bluntly, to pronounce it directly and without hedging, in my own personal view, myself, personally, I think taxes suck."

I exaggerate a tad here for effect, but it pales beside the mountains of unnecessary verbiage common to too many speeches in too many scripts.

The point is: Get to the point!

There is positively no excuse for having a character begin a line of dialogue with "I think." We can take it as given that anything any character says he also thinks. No line of dialogue that begins with "I think" cannot be improved by lopping off those first two words.

Another common problem is the vocalized pause, "Well."

Rich Little, impersonator of celebrities, once described how he worked out his Ronald Reagan impression. Reagan, he explained, begins virtually every single utterance with "Well." Little, having performed at Reagan's inauguration, eventually received a telegram from the White House expressing the President's appreciation. "Even the telegram," notes the comic, "opened with 'Well.' "

"You know" is another major problem both in speech and in writing. Needless to say, any screenwriter who uses the phrase "you know" should be promptly and summarily drummed out of the union.

Real life conversations overflow with these blunted openings and nervous, useless interjections. There's no excuse for them in movie scripts. The conversations created by artists require choice, discrimination, selection, and every bit as important, *de*selection between that which is worthy and that which is not.

Exclude Dialect

Dialogue and dialect are completely separate enterprises.

Throughout his career, John Wayne patently refused to read screenplays containing slangy, twangy, lazy, yawning, shucks, gee-whiz, gosh-all-mighty jargon transliterated by writers presuming to impress him. They impressed him, all right, but not in the way they intended. Wayne didn't need writers to drop his *g*'s for him. He portrayed roles precisely in the manner of John Wayne, and all he required of writers was that they write skillfully and in English.

Writers most commonly fall into the dialect trap when crafting foreign, ethnic, and racial roles. In real life, for example, middle-class white Americans commonly pronounce *going* and *coming* as *goin'* and *comin'*, yet screenwriters typically drop the *g*'s in their scripts exclusively for down-and-dirty poverty-struck folk, particularly disadvantaged blacks, which smacks of bigotry.

Filmmaking, to reiterate, consists of collaboration among artists. Instead of futilely resisting that special aspect of the medium, screenwriters ought to embrace it. Let the actors and the director seek the most effective way to deliver the dialogue. Write "Badges? We don't need no stinking badges," and leave it to the actor to pronounce it, "Botches? We doh nee no steenking botches."

While there is always the possibility the collaborators will botch it, they may actually make it even better than the writer imagined it could be. In any case, the writer's choice is severely limited in the matter. By attempting to direct the entire film from behind the keys of his typewriter, he can only restrict the script's chances to soar.

Use the Rhythm Method

Material written to be read aloud is vastly different from material written merely to be read.

Some years ago I had dinner with some old film school pals and our spouses. Happily, members of the group had by then already established themselves as responsible and respectable film professionals. Before dinner we all sat around in the living room quaffing wine, gobbling cheese, chitchattering away with a distinct tilt toward film-phony show biz babble. How's Bruce's project at Fox? Did Gary close his deal at CBS? Does Paul have final cut on his picture for Lorimar? Has Steve changed agents for the third time this month?

The hosts' daughter was then not quite two. During the continuing cocktail conversation, Mother trotted out the child, set her in the center of the rug amidst the group, and retreated to the kitchen. After the obligatory chorus of ooohing and aahing, the conversation drifted back to the standard, hollow, upscale patter. All the while the child, now largely unnoticed, stared with soft, dark, wide, all-absorbing eyes at the circle of adults, scanning, tracking them like radar with her gaze. Perhaps some twenty minutes later Mom reappeared, plucked the child from the carpet, and took her away to her crib.

Moments later, the group was summoned to dinner. Thanks to the wine, I was moved to visit the powder room before taking my seat at the table. Moving along the hall, I happened to pass the open door of the little girl's room. And the sound emanating from that room stopped me cold, filled me with wonder and awe.

It was not much more than a quiet yammering, a bubbling, gurgling chant, a child's preverbal mantra. Yet it was also the fully faithful playback of the entire conversation that had just transpired in the other room! The girl could only imitate language in a crude, primitive manner, trafficking essentially in echolalia, the unstructured, wordless babble of babies. Nevertheless, unerringly she captured the overall effect, the gestalt, most especially the rhythm of the adults' chatter. Without a word of actual language, here were all the rising and falling inflections, the anxious, soaring interrogatories, the grunting, assertive affirmations, hedging vocalized pauses, queries and responses, couched denials, declarations and rejoinders, all the gags and giggles that had occurred in the living room only minutes earlier.

It told more of the basic nature of human verbal interchange than any fifty film-writing texts. It is virtually impossible to reproduce the sound in print but it was one hundred percent rhythm—dit dit dah? Dah *dah!* Dit dah? Dah! Dah dah *dah.*

That's what movie dialogue is—not real speech, but the overall *effect* of real speech.

Real speech is available free of charge in the streets. Dialogue, on the other hand, is worth waiting in line for. It needs to be special. Unless it writhes and wriggles, glows and glistens, it is unworthy of any audience.

Remember that all language is a kind of song containing words and music, sentences hooking into each other with beats and pauses that follow lyrically. Tension constantly needs to be created and then promptly resolved.

Don't Underscore

Inexperienced writers, overly anxious to communicate their dialogue's subtlety, tend to underscore entire speeches, even whole scenes.

But a well-crafted line of dialogue ought to contain within its own context natural locations for emphasis. "You talking to me?" as spoken by protagonist Travis Bickle in *Taxi Driver* is all screenwriter Paul Schrader had to write; he did not need to write: "You talking to *me*?"

From time to time, in this line or that, places for such emphasis may well vary. But again, unless it is critical to the plot, unless there is some precise, integrated justification for its use, writers are well advised to avoid underscoring. They should grant actors and directors full freedom to find the most effective, appropriate locations for emphasis.

Where did Shakespeare underscore?

Nowhere.

Does this handicap an actor's ability to read a Shakespearean role? Absolutely not. Centuries of arguments regarding locations for emphasis testify not to his weakness but to his strength.

When writers indiscriminately underscore, instead of punching, highlighting, or emphasizing a word or a line, they squander its impact and blunt the usefulness of underscoring in those rare instances when the practice actually possesses value.

... Avoid ... Ellipses

If screenwriters underscore more frequently than they should, they are positively ellipsis-mad.

An ellipsis is a series of three dots intended to represent omitted words not necessary to understanding. One such occurrence is an ellipsis; two are ellipses; three are three more than required.

Ellipses represent a plague on screenplays.

In his gross and grossly underrated *History of the World, Part 1,* Mel Brooks actually has a character pronounce the ellipses—"dot, dot, dot, I, dot, dot, dot, don't know, dot, dot, dot, what to say, dot, dot, dot, dot."

There are probably two reasons why inexperienced screenwriters are so fond of the device. First, in keeping with their naive and futile mania not merely to write but to direct the entire film from their typewriters, writers often wish to compel actors to pause or hesitate when they deem appropriate. Yet in context, effectively honed dialogue conveys such pauses naturally. Crafty dialogue invites the actor to discover the emotion on his own. He might even invent some nuance superior to that which the writer intended. A heartfelt confession, for example, might most effectively be spoken simply, quietly, in a straightforward fashion, without a lot of histrionic mumbling through a minefield of dots.

The second reason screenwriters underscore too frequently is because they are cowards. Rather than assert themselves, purposefully and deliberately finishing a sentence with a good old-fashioned period, many prefer to trail off, deflate like a leaky tire. I have read entire screenplays in which not a single speech ends with a period.

Remember, to write a screenplay is to play God. Each writer creates the universe of his own screenplay. Does the all-knowing King of the Universe hedge his bets? Of course not. Does He equivocate? Never.

And neither should you.

Is there any place at all where ellipses may properly be used?

Yes.

When one character starts a sentence that another finishes, as if the latter were attempting to head off an unpleasant truth he expects the former to reveal, ellipses connecting the two incomplete lines—ending the first, beginning the second—are perfectly legitimate.

For example:

> HARRY
> Sarah's age? Why, she's ...

> SARAH
> ... thirty-nine.

Avoid Parenthetical Directions

Parenthetical directions are those little legends enclosed in parentheses directly below a character's name and immediately above the dialogue. They usually contain information about the dialogue's delivery.

For example:

> HARRY
> Sarah's age? Why, she's ...

> SARAH
> (interrupting)
> ... thirty nine.

Usually, as above, they are unnecessary. They add no new information. Remember, a good script is good characters in a good story, conveyed through sight and sound. When writers gratuitously provide a catalogue of precise parenthetical instructions regarding the manner in which dialogue should be read, it is not merely unappreciated, it is resented. The extra verbiage makes the script harder to read. And the parentheticals intrude upon other artists' territories, inhibiting their ability to collaborate productively.

Readers, actors, and audiences ought to be seduced into a tale by a script's skill, the writer's finesse with people and plot. Instead of brazenly stating, resourceful writers imply. They thereby require readers to participate actively, to use their own heads to draw themselves closer to the tale. Spoon-feeding, spelling out every nuance, distances rather than attracts the reader.

The first thing an actor does when he receives a script from a movie or television producer is to cross out all of his character's parenthetical directions. And in many screenplays that is quite a task, as there are scripts where every single line is accompanied by just such prescription. The writer commands one line's delivery to be "joyful," the next "happy," the one after that "gleeful."

Inventing a good story with good characters is hard enough work without struggling to find synonyms that never needed to be written in the first place. The situation, the context, the scene itself should compel the line's emotion. What's more, it's good creative fun to explore different deliveries of lines.

In *Play Misty for Me,* for example, a deranged fan harasses a disc jockey, relentlessly stalking him. At one point she confronts him in his convertible, yanking his keys from the ignition, then retreating just a few steps beyond his reach. He politely yet firmly requests the return of the keys. Dangling them in the air, the woman's response is something on the order of: "You want them? Here they are. Come and get them."

This line in the screenplay contains the parenthetical direction: (livid with rage).

But with what else can one be livid if not rage? Halvah?

"Livid," all by itself, is more than sufficient. But even excluding "with rage," the parenthetical direction remains useless.

On screen, the actress chooses to read the line in a wholly different manner. Instead of foaming at the mouth with fathomless anger, grunting, growling like the Satan-possessed girl in *The Exorcist,* she speaks the words brightly, perkily, almost as if coaxing a puppy to frolic with a new toy. That the line is delivered so matter-of-factly, so down-right cheerily, provides a grim counterpoint to her rage and reveals how crazy she truly is. Her unearthly calm betrays her fury. The lethal passion, implied instead of expressed, forces the audience to project its own rage and experience the passion far more keenly.

The writer of *Play Misty for Me* is fortunate to have had an actress sufficiently secure to ignore the script's parenthetical restrictions. If the writer's orders had been followed to the letter, the film would have been less effective.

Shakespeare utilized parenthetical directions exactly nowhere throughout his collected plays. Far from limiting performance and interpretation, opportunities for both were vastly enhanced.

Given inexperienced writers' penchant for littering their scripts with a surplus of parenthetical directions, I find myself more than a little reluctant to volunteer that here and there legitimate occasions for their use do in fact exist. As ever, the test is integration. If the parenthetical instruction offers new and necessary information, writers ought to use it. A common use involves scenes with several characters, where it is unclear on the page precisely who says what to whom. If Bruno, Harriet, and Charles are deciding who will drive the getaway car in their bank heist, it might serve to direct the dialogue parenthetically. Otherwise, we don't know whom Bruno addresses.

                    BRUNO
                 (to Harry)
         You drive the getaway car.

A common mistake writers make with parenthetical directions is using them to describe visual action and business.

> BRUNO
> (picking up the gun, mopping his brow
> with his handkerchief, gesturing toward
> the door)
> Let's get out of here.

As with so many techniques, parenthetical directions can be of great value, but only if used sparingly.

Avoid *#?@>?* Funny *!‾1]}!*! Punctuation!!!

Take a look at the comics in today's newspaper. Virtually every line of dialogue that is not a question ends with an exclamation point. So, if you want your screenplay to look like a comic, recklessly spray exclamation points throughout its breadth and length.

Otherwise, leave them out.

As with underscoring and parenthetical directions, a line's intent, import, and subtext ought to emerge from the situation and the words. Limp lines can't be rendered perky with wild squiggles, dots, and slashes.

Avoid Long Speeches

In real life people do not make long, unwieldy speeches to each other. Neither should they in films.

Movies prefer natural-sounding, quick, short, to-the-point dialogue with lines that link, interlock, intertwine, and bounce up and back like a Ping-Pong ball among the characters. Respectable professional dialogue possesses a sense of give and take, questions, answers, hooks, eyes, a sing-song flow, and an underlying seductive rhythm that is somehow at once pleasing yet disquieting.

Clearly, this is easier to demand than it is to create.

How to achieve it?

Carefully.

Write, rewrite, rewrite again. And again.

Before reading a script, the vast preponderance of agents and producers give it to a professional analyst for a written summary and appraisal. Before the reader studies the manuscript he flips through it. Even this superficial skimming quickly reveals whether the screenplay is saturated with lengthy speeches. If there are interchanges of soliloquies instead of effective, efficient, snappy, peppy dialogue, this becomes immediately apparent, thanks to the blocky look imparted by all those speeches.

If you want your script instantaneously to be pegged as amateurish, be sure to cram it with such speeches.

Argue

Even if you avoid having your script become a catalogue of bulky, blocky speeches, it is still not sufficient merely to have characters trade quips, no matter how clever and crisp such banter may be.

Let your characters argue. Let each line challenge the next.

Don't let anybody agree with anybody else; as soon as there is agreement there is boredom. There is, of course, a difference between toe-to-toe, eyeball-to-eyeball argument and mere bickering. But if your characters perpetually oppose one another through argument, the script will forever contain conflict without ever truly achieving resolution until the one and only place within a screenplay where resolution is to be tolerated: the end.

A writer contemplating dialogue craft could do a lot worse than to imagine himself in a public place—for example a park or restaurant—in close proximity to a couple of strangers who are in the midst of conversation. If they're peaceful, agreeable, if their collective effect is flat, there is no inclination to eavesdrop. But should the exchange turn angry and argumentative, people will quickly strain to overhear.

Indeed, writers are well advised to view their entire screenplay as one extended, endless argument from start to finish.

Note that throughout this chapter purporting exclusively to treat dialogue, we've touched inevitably upon a whole host of assorted screenwriting subjects: story (the Strangler); conflict (argument); and others. This is all further testimony to screenwriting's integration. For it is impossible to discuss one aspect of film writing without connecting it to others. This demonstrates once again that film's truest value resides not in its scattered elements but in the way the elements integrate into the whole picture.

And among all these scattered elements collectively comprising a film, dialogue is of critical importance. While story, theme, and character are more immediate considerations confronting screenwriters, the medium by which these primary elements are communicated to audiences is largely dialogue.

Skillfully crafted dialogue shouldn't show. That is to say, it must sound as if the actors thought it up all by themselves. Audiences know better, of course, but they are entitled to the illusion that somehow the characters knew just what to say and when to say it. And screenwriters need also remember that the best dialogue is often no dialogue at all.

6

ACTION AND SETTING:

Little Things

Mean a Lot

The word *drama* derives from the Greek term meaning "to do; to act."

Film and television drama does not merely require, therefore, that among all its various elements there is also action. Drama *is* action. What drama is *not* is a bunch of characters sitting around talking, twiddling their thumbs, doing nothing.

Among screenwriters' most central challenges then is, first, to determine for each scene what action most effectively advances the story and expands the characters and, second, what is the ideal setting for that action.

Two clear principles can be quickly established: (1) any action is better than no action, and (2) appropriate imaginative, integrated action, action complementing a scene's other elements and overall purpose, is best of all.

Most obvious among film's unique characteristics is its ability to depict experiences and settings of such enormous sweep as to defy representation in any other medium. A skyscraper afire in a film appears very much to be a skyscraper afire; on stage it can be merely suggested. An ocean liner capsized on film looks just like an ocean liner capsized at sea; on stage it can be merely represented through an inventory of clues.

But what film really does best is not render that which is big still bigger; far more important, it makes that which is little seem big. It makes the personal, intimate moment available to masses of viewers. And it accomplishes this with a facility simply not possible in theatrical drama or any other format.

Throughout the middle and late sixties some of the most human, most courageous films came out of Czechoslovakia. Tragically, this creative flurry was abruptly stifled by the Soviet occupation of August 1968. Among the more outstanding of these movies is *Loves of a Blonde,* a film containing one scene in particular that is at once painful and hilarious.

Two separate groups of laborers—one male, the other female—at work on a project in a remote section of the Carpathian foothills are brought together to dine in a common hall. Like overage adolescents, the men-starved women and the women-starved men are all excruciatingly nervous about meeting one another.

The camera closes in on one man in particular who fusses distractedly with his wedding ring. Unexpectedly, it slips from his finger, landing on the floor with a loud clang. Was he mindlessly fidgeting, or did he subconsciously intend to remove the ring to conceal from the women the fact that he is married?

He drops to the floor in pursuit of the ring, and the camera drops with him, following him beneath the table, past row after row of knees, chasing the elusive rolling band. Soon, unbeknownst to him, the knees are no longer those of men but of women. And when at last he emerges from beneath the tables triumphantly lofting the ring, to his chagrin he finds himself standing among the very group of people from whom he was trying to conceal his marital status in the first place—the women.

Here is a physically small, emotionally huge, logistically precise event capable of depiction on film alone; on stage it could no more easily be conveyed than a plague of locusts. It is something film treats to full and brilliant effect.

The screenwriter who structures such a scene exploits film's richest capabilities. He is inventive, fresh. And so should be all screenwriters.

Ironically, this prescription may well confront writers with an apparent inconsistency, for earlier I warned that detailed visual action—everything in a screenplay besides dialogue—is often characterized by producers and other readers as "all that black stuff," often merely skimmed if not skipped completely. But this is in fact no reason to favor talky scripts over true *pictures*. The trick is first of all to select delicate, fine details appropriate to the film's story, and then to describe them economically, without wasting a lot of language.

Avoid Static Situations

Settings, along with every other aspect of screenplays, should be integrated and fluid; they should be fresh and unexpected instead of familiar, and conducive to action taking place within them. Set a scene at an Internal Revenue Service tax audit, in a church confessional, at a gymnasium. And avoid settings that are patent excuses to cover up the fact that the dialogue is *instead* of action. If the scene's import can be gleaned with the projector's bulb burned out, there is a need for greater invention and imagination on the part of the writer.

Telephones

Why do so many films and television shows contain so many scenes with so many folks squawking on the phone? No doubt it's because writers in a hurry, bereft of energy and imagination, seize upon the phone as a quick, cheap way to have actors tell the tale through talk instead of acting it out through action.

An actress of substantial experience, much of it in television, recently commented that the greatest breakthrough for performers was not Stanislavsky; it is the touch-tone telephone. She swears the index finger of her right hand has grown measurably shorter as a result of dialing so many phones in so many drab, unimaginative scenes. The advent of touch-tone dialing at least enables her to get the dialing over with much more quickly, and saves her a small fortune in manicures.

If you positively must have a scene on the phone, make it special, see that it is integrated as in John Guare's *Atlantic City*. Here, a figure slinks into a telephone booth, pretends to dial but quickly hangs up, runs his hands atop the phone, locates a mysterious package, tucks it under his arm, and hastily departs. Almost immediately thereafter a second figure appears in the booth. He, too, feels around as if for a package and appears dismayed to discover there is none.

Here is a phone scene with no dialogue at all! Much story and character freight is transported wholly via visual imagery and physical action. It sure beats having to watch actors read lines into a telephone.

But if for some reason characters absolutely must speak on the phone, make it special. There is a scene, for example, in the comedy *My Favorite Year* in which the youthful protagonist telephones his home in Brooklyn to announce that he is bringing a world-famous movie star to have dinner with the family. The excited shenanigans in the background are grand fun. An aunt, for instance, wanting to wear her fanciest garment, puts on nothing less than her wedding dress. The call's craziness is not only funny, although that alone would surely warrant its place in the film; more important, it advances the story and expands our knowledge of the characters.

Cars

So many movies have so many scenes in which characters endlessly drive around in cars that I have often wondered why the motion-sickness remedy Dramamine isn't sold alongside the popcorn and Milk Duds at movie theater candy counters.

Again, a scene in a car, like any scene at all, is tolerable if it is also integrated, that is, if it moves not only passengers but also story and character. Not surprisingly, most often it's merely one more cheap, easy way to have the tale told via talk instead of action, with scenery streaming by providing a substitute for genuine action.

So try to avoid having characters drive around, chatting up the tale. Integrate it into the story if you can, as in the scene from *Close Encounters of the Third Kind,* where Richard Dreyfuss stops his truck to check the map, only to have the lights of the flying saucer pull up behind him. Clearly believing it is merely another automobile, he absently signals for it to pass, which it does, directly over the roof of his pickup.

Restaurants and Bars

For the same reason films are phone-crazy and car-crazy, they are also saturated with drab scenes set in restaurants and bars. Such settings may offer facile ways to provide actors with physical business—mixing drinks, wielding knives and forks—but after all is said and done such scenes expose the tale not through action but through dialogue.

The same actress who hailed the touch-tone telephone complains that in her considerable career she has by now mixed tens of thousands of gallons of cocktails. Once again such activity offers the appearance of action beyond mere talk, but such business is not truly integrated into story and character. It is but an attempt—and a transparent one at that—to mask the fact that the tale is being revealed solely through dialogue.

If a writer must have a scene in a restaurant, let it be like that in *The Idolmaker.* Here writer Edward DiLorenzo gives us a brother, brilliantly portrayed by Ray Sharkey, reluctant to accept from his hoodlum father money intended for launching a new business venture. The confrontation is held in a restaurant, but it is not just any restaurant. Indeed, it is the restaurant owned by the younger brother, the "good" brother, to which he was staked by the father. What's more, the Sharkey character has already been seen at picture's opening working as a waiter at the same restaurant, testifying still further to the setting's and action's integration into the film's most basic structure.

Sharkey and the audience, viewing the father's abuse of the younger brother, are made to appreciate the protagonist's tension should he, too, consent to his father's support. Character and tale are expanded in a single stroke.

In the film *About Last Night* there is a scene set in a diner. The diner is run-down, decrepit. Later on in the tale the protagonist takes over the diner, restores it, revitalizes it, turns it into a thriving business. It becomes the vehicle of his liberation. It is a metaphor for his seizing control of his life. And it is perfectly justifiable, therefore, to play out certain scenes in such a setting because, again, these scenes, like the diner itself, are integrated into the tale, advancing the audience's appreciation of the characters.

That's a far cry from cheap excuses for providing actors with mundane business to cover the fact that all they're really doing is talking.

Hotels, Apartments, Offices

There is in movies a lamentable glut of hotels, apartments, and offices. Surely, sometimes such settings are justified. Television series set in the home will invariably play out—where else?—in the home. But as with all other aspects of screenwriting, writers should struggle to make such settings count for something, impart to them a measure of integration.

In the first draft of a UCLA student's romantic thriller there were three separate scenes played out in the protagonist's hotel room. Rewriting, he left one scene in the room, moved the second to a hot tub, and the third to a subway car. This may not represent boundless genius, but it surely expands the film, providing a richer view and more widely varied experiences for an audience.

In another student's police drama there was a scene in which the protagonist, a lieutenant on the force, confronts his captain. In the first draft, the scene played out in the captain's office. In the second draft, the same scene was moved to a swimming pool. The captain, on orders from his physician to exercise, has taken to swimming instead of eating lunch. And so virtually the identical scene plays out at poolside, with the captain swimming up and back as the lieutenant walks alongside atop the pool's deck, shouting the conversation at him.

It's a whole lot more fun than sitting around in yet one more office. And far more than just plain fun, it underscores the captain's competitive nature, the somewhat humiliating need for the lieutenant to tolerate his superior officer's quirks, and the lieutenant's general compulsion doggedly to go along in order to get along. Dialogue, action, and setting are united into a single entity that effectively and inexorably moves all of the film's elements in tandem, as if they were one—which, in good films, is precisely what they are.

Give the Actors Something to Do

Setting the scene with the captain and lieutenant at poolside does more than merely open it up. It provides the actors with real physical business.

The captain gets to swim up and back, gasping, wheezing his dialogue. The lieutenant at poolside has far richer opportunities to flesh out his character, shouting at the captain in order to be heard above the din, dodging the splashes and puddles, slipping and sliding on the shiny, hard tiles. A raw tale is transformed into a feast of integrated details.

All by itself this will not make a lousy movie good, but at the very least it makes an okay movie better. Broad, fertile environments are available to writers if only they will reach, stretch, invent, instead of rehashing the same old settings.

In *The Rose Tattoo* a scene is set in a hotel room in

which Anna Magnani confronts her lover. But the room is not just any hotel room—it is a hellhole with a tiny sink against one wall.

Magnani rinses out her stockings. She wrings them dry as only she could wring them, with that special, painful Mediterranean angst. The action symbolizes the relationship, which is wrung every bit as dry. Now she strings a cord across the room and hangs the stockings to dry. The scene, which might otherwise consist solely of two actors swapping lines in some dull setting, becomes instead a feast of sight and sound and action, all of it integrated into character and story.

On a recent episode of television's treasured *St. Elsewhere,* three of the ensemble players find themselves riding an elevator together. They try on each other's glasses and comment upon their respective myopia as well as the cosmetic appearance of the various frames. All of this is small business made big. Significantly, the particular episode in which this scene appears addresses issues of vision and blindness, further evidence of solid story integration.

Another splendid example of little things made big is found in *Kramer vs. Kramer.* When the first morning arrives and Mother has not yet returned, for once in his life Dad has to prepare breakfast for his kid. No big deal, right? Women make such a federal case out of these petty domestic ceremonies. Dad can easily enough cook up a respectable breakfast for his son as effectively as Mom ever did. And never mind cornflakes in a bowl with milk. The kid can have whatever he wants.

And what does he want?

French toast.

No problem. But no sooner does father stride into the kitchen than he discovers he's as lost there as in the jungles of Borneo. Where are the bowls? Where are the eggs? Where's the bread, the butter, the sugar, the milk? Where's a whisk to beat the stuff? Instead of a proper mixing bowl, Dad prepares the concoction in a drinking glass, which wrecks the bread.

Kramer is seen to be a stranger in a strange land. Screenwriter Robert Benton, adapting Avery Corman's novel, invests with monumental tension the mundane act of preparing French toast. It illuminates the protagonist's characteristics far more eloquently than the sharpest, snappiest, crispest, most brittle banter and repartee.

And at film's end, when Kramer once again prepares French toast, we see that he now knows precisely how to do it. He whisks the eggs with the proper whisk, in the proper stainless steel bowl. He wields pots and pans with the elegance and finesse of a master chef. The simple, close-up, everyday act of preparing his young son's breakfast offers eloquent testimony to his fulfillment as a father, as a man.

Such little, ordinary, everyday actions magnify films, render them enormous, enable them satisfyingly to fill a broad screen in a vast, cavernous theater. Writers need vigorously and imaginatively to seek out these details, big and little, to create them, in order to tell their tale most effectively and to paint portraits of the characters who inhabit them.

Integration

What precisely is the principle by which a writer determines actions and settings appropriate to particular moments in his script? It is the same as with virtually every other aspect of screenwriting: integration. He chooses those actions and settings that uniquely synchronize with everything else in the film.

In *WarGames* the protagonist, a young computer hacker, is locked in a sterile chamber deep within the underground military command headquarters. How shall he escape? By surprising a guard and beating him over the head? We've seen that hundreds of times in thousands of movies. By removing the acoustical tiles in the ceiling and slipping through the air-conditioning ducts? Again, even if it is marginally acceptable, it is hardly original. And in no event is such action especially appropriate to this character in this setting.

Instead, by use of his miniature tape recorder, he surreptitiously records the beeping musical code a guard uses to unlock the door. Later, alone, he plays the same recording back to the locking device, which obediently snaps open. Why is this the best choice? Integration. The kid is a computer expert. The whole movie is built around his having penetrated the national security computer network. Clearly, a computer-oriented scheme for his escape, one utilizing his already established microchip skills, best suits the whole film.

In *The Godfather* a rich man defies the mob. How shall they punish him? Burn down his house? Implant an ice pick in his temple? Both? Perhaps these are workable after a fashion, but are they truly integrated? Are they fresh? Are they special to this character in this setting?

Definitely not. Instead, hooking into the previously established fact that the character is especially fond of a champion racehorse he owns, the writer has the man awake in his sumptuous silk-sheeted bed to discover his prize steed's bloody head beside him.

In *Atlantic City* John Guare creates a scene in which a beautiful young woman stands in her kitchen stripped to the waist, gently, lingeringly massaging her breasts with fresh lemon juice. I admit I don't mind one bit viewing such a scene even merely for its own sake; as discussed in the chapter on conflict, eroticism has been a central component of drama since its earliest days on the ancient Greek stage, even if in those years the actors kept their clothes on. But is this scene particularly appropriate to this film?

Yes, absolutely. The same woman has been shown earlier to hold a crummy job serving fried fish at a fast food joint. The fish odor permeates her every pore, serves as a metaphor for her disenchantment with her life, her frustration and self-contempt. The lemon juice treatment offers a humble opportunity even temporarily to cleanse herself of this rancid reminder of her sorry station. Sure, it's erotic, but it's also much more than that. It properly integrates the movie's other scenes and actions. It isn't merely added on; it is elegantly woven into the film's fabric.

The challenge, then, in choosing actions and settings that are truly exquisite instead of merely serviceable, is for writers to look to the rest of their film. In story, character, theme, within the whole body of collective actions they should find clues to direct them toward those inventions that are different from the usual material we see in every other movie, and that uniquely fit a particular film at a particular moment.

If action defines character, then character defines action. To determine what action a character should take and in what setting, the writer should study the character. Action and character, combined with dialogue and placed in the properly integrated setting, add up to screenwriting's single most important element: story.

7

FORMAT:

Sight and Sound

Compared to crafting a solid story filled with worthy characters speaking crisp, tale-wagging dialogue, setting a screenplay in proper, professional format is easier than tying your shoes.

Nevertheless, in keeping with screenwriting's schizophrenic nature, format is at the same time extremely important. This is true first of all because it serves as a measure of a writer's appreciation for the way he comes across, and second because it serves also as a tool for rendering screenplays as readable as the form allows. And readability can be an elusive quantity in screenplays. (Many of the items in this chapter are more easily understood by referring now and again to the sample screenplay page at the chapter's end.)

As asserted earlier, for all its complexity a movie provides but two kinds of information: sight and sound. All aspects of a screenplay—story, character, action, setting, and everything else—derive from what an audience sees and hears.

This requires that screenwriters work backward. After conjuring up images in his mind, the writer puts words on paper in such a manner as to cause the reader to see in his own mind something closely resembling the writer's original vision. This is no mean feat. Its success depends upon the writer utilizing his imagination and discipline most skillfully, so that from sight and sound alone characters' internal thoughts are exposed to a viewing, listening audience.

In Ernest Lehman's screenplay *North by Northwest,* there is a celebrated scene in which Cary Grant, standing innocently in the United Nations lobby, suddenly finds collapsed in his arms the limp body of a stranger who, moments earlier, stood beside him. Grant, discovering a knife handle protruding from his late neighbor's back, reflexively withdraws it, at which point, naturally, news photographers' bulbs flash.

The image, soon to appear on front pages across the nation, of Grant holding the knife over the victim's bloody back, is distinctly incriminating. A novelist could simply write that the character realizes he appears very much to be the culprit. In a film, however, this information can be made manifest only through a clever combination of images and sounds: events, action, expressions on characters' faces, lines of dialogue, sound effects.

Format, then, is in fact no more complicated than placing the sound—mainly dialogue—in one place and the sight—action, settings—in another. In the United States the former occupies narrow margins forming a column down the center of the page; the latter is assigned wider margins, border to border the breadth of the page.

The limitations of sight and sound require that a screenwriter never write what a character "thinks," "realizes," "recalls," or "remembers," nor what he "figures" or "calculates," for these are in their nature internal, mental processes, which in screenplays are communicated by sight and sound alone.

This requirement to present such information visually is one reason that the screenplay, contrary to popular misconception, represents a more demanding form of writing than the novel.

Interestingly, many screenwriters—and no small number of other film professionals—reject this notion. But this only testifies to Hollywood's long-standing inferiority complex where the screenplay is viewed as a lower species of creative expression. A novel's readers can pick it up and put it down as they see fit; they control the pace at which the material is absorbed. They can skim this part, or skip it altogether. They can reread that other part forty times if it suits them. But a movie cranks at twenty-four frames per second for everybody. For this reason it is wholly intolerant of inefficiency, totally unforgiving of poor economy.

Happily, if screenwriters are faithful to the limitations of sight and sound they can get away with paying almost no attention to format whatever; they can write their scripts any which way and then hire typists to set them in the proper margins. And indeed, as indicated in the section on word processing in Part III, The Writing Habit, within minutes computer programs can transform a near-random script into a properly formatted one.

While far less critical than story and character, format is nonetheless important to screenwriters in two ways. First, clear formatting testifies to a screenwriter's professionalism even before the script is read. Second, effective formatting is itself a creative tool useful to writers eager to paint their portraits and depict their plots in an articulate, imaginative fashion.

There is not and never has been an official, authorized screenplay format. Formats vary among production styles: standard theatrical feature films, three-camera taped television, documentary. They vary also within forms; writers utilize format creatively to assert their personal style and taste. And formats vary among nations. This book deals for the most part with the American theatrical feature-length film.

As a writer and educator I am constantly approached by people seeking to codify the screenplay format, to determine once and for all precisely what the margin and tab settings shall be, what terms shall be upper case and lower, where if anywhere to place the *continued*'s, whether to number the scenes, where and when to specify camera angles, plus a host of other considerations.

But I reject the notion that my position confers upon me any such authority. Writers ought to be free to manipulate format in whatever ways they believe will enhance their script's clarity. There is no good purpose in restricting screenwriters' capacity to invent, to be original, and for that matter to fall flat on their faces, even merely so far as format is concerned.

All of the rules and examples that follow, therefore, should be taken with not merely a grain but a truckload of salt; I urge writers to reject them freely, to run roughshod over them, to take responsibility for their own writing, to modify screenplay format in as many ways as they see fit in the effort to make their scripts readable.

No High-Tech Jargon

Compared to novels, compared to poems, even excellent screenplays can be a chore to read. For in the purest sense, screenplays are not meant to be read at all so much as they are intended to be filmed. Cutting up and back between snatches of dialogue, description, action, and business, the endless smattering of shots, angles, and set-ups inevitably renders even a good script rather a burden both to eye and to brain.

Every screenwriter should write in such a fashion as to make it possible for any intelligent reader to understand and, if at all possible, even to enjoy his script. To this end, fancy film-technical jargon—lenses, angles, effects, tilts, pans, trucks, zooms, the entire array of camera moves, the whole glossary of film tech talk—is to be avoided except in those rare instances when it is absolutely necessary for a specific reason that can be readily explained or when it is inextricably integrated into advancing both character and tale.

The purpose of a screenplay, simply stated, is to convey

to readers the movie playing in the writer's head. The author imagines a movie; he describes it in words on pages. The reader reads the pages. Ideally, from the words on the pages the reader forms in his own head a movie closely resembling the one playing inside that of the writer.

That's the task.

And it's no easy task, for writer *or* reader. A common mistake is the assumption that the greater the number of words used to explain a particular scene, the clearer its meaning. In fact the opposite is true. As writers ramble on and on, endlessly detailing this item and that one, the action becomes increasingly clouded by the swarming verbiage.

Face it: A sunset is a sunset. On film it will be as plain or as beautiful as the one available on the particular day it is scheduled to be filmed. If in his script the writer calls for a sunset that is "maroonish, streaked with amber, a touch of lingering cyan, with just a hint of magenta," the crew will not wait around for a sunset that fits the description on the page. They'll shoot the sunset God throws at them the day they set up to shoot it. Indeed, if it suits a production's schedule, they'll shoot the dawn, run it backward, and on screen declare it to be sunset.

Writers who squander language not only make their scripts intensely more difficult to read; subliminally they communicate that readers need not pay close attention to what is written, as there are obvious conceits quickly to be discarded upon production. If a writer wishes his script to be closely attended, he better be certain everything in it is worth attending.

Do not, therefore, write for the cinematographer, or for the editor, or the chief electrician, gaffer, first/second assistant director. Write instead for any literate person, and then all the technicians, agents, actors, and producers will easily follow the drama mounted in your screenplay.

Master Scenes Only

Even the briefest scene in a screenplay, when projected upon the screen, likely contains dozens of separate shots.

Say one character, a spy, meets another at a hot dog stand, exchanges documents, cash, and quick conversation, then departs. On screen there might well appear first a wide shot of the stand, a reverse angle on the approaching character, a closer shot of the contact, perhaps close-ups of the cash, the documents. Within the conversation there would likely be several two-shots containing both characters, plus various over-the-shoulder singles—close-up images of each character's face alone in the frame as seen from the other character's point of view—speaking, reacting.

Additionally, there would likely be cutaways to peripheral characters and sights: the vendor smearing mustard on a hot dog, the sizzling grill, pigeons pecking at crumbs, another customer downing a soft drink, a bag lady poking through the garbage in search of spent aluminum cans.

These glances provide much color and realism to a movie, but the screenwriter who indicates every one of these shots in his script commits a serious error. First, shattering the scene into a blizzard of separate shots certainly makes it far more difficult to read compared to a single master scene. Second, breaking up a scene, indeed an entire script into all of its various shots, is actually the editor's task. And the editor enjoys having the writer do his work for him about as much as the writer enjoys the producer's manicurist's cousin's mailman's dentist "touching up" his dialogue.

Instead of a flurry of fragmented images, one broad, all-encompassing view of the setting—a master scene—is preferred. In the hypothetical spy scene above, the writer needs merely to call the widest shot—HOT DOG STAND—and provide the handful of essential details: characters, basic action succinctly described, and the dialogue.

A note of caution: I constantly urge writers to read as many scripts as they can find. If they do this, however, they are likely to see scripts—among them some of the most splendid—that do not look anything at all like master-scene scripts. But writers need be aware that they may very well be looking at a so-called shooting script, one that has been prepared at the last moment immediately prior to production so that the director knows precisely how much coverage is required, how many angles, how much specific and technical detail needs to be filmed.

The writer may or may not be involved in the preparation of this final version. But whether he is or is not, he needs to concentrate not upon the shooting script, but the showcase script, the master-scene script, that early draft clearly depicting the essential action and dialogue, with just enough ruffles and flourishes to allow him to establish his own personal style.

Increasingly these days it is becoming possible to obtain actual screenplays from a variety of sources. What's more, there are greater numbers of screenplays being published. Readers need to be cautious, however, as published screenplays are frequently offered in incorrect format. William Goldman's *Adventures in the Screen Trade,* mentioned in the "Recommended Reading" at the end of this book, contains his somewhat unconventionally formatted script for *Butch Cassidy and the Sundance Kid.* It's worth a look. And Brian Henderson's *Five Screenplays by Sturges Preston,* similarly listed, contains no fewer than five screenplays in their original format.

Numbers—(1) Pages, (2) Drafts, (3) Dates, (4) Scenes

Naturally, a screenwriter ought to number the pages in his script. But he should not number his drafts or his scenes, nor should he include any reference—on the cover, the title page, or elsewhere—to the date of the writing.

Pages

First, regarding pages, it is most important that the total number falls within professional limits. Though there are variations, a typical screenplay page translates into approximately a minute of screen time. In the golden age of Hollywood—the 1930s and 1940s—when the typical movie fare included newsreels, short subjects, cartoons, coming attractions, and finally not one but two full features, pictures were understandably shorter. Many ran not much more than an hour; seventy-five or eighty minutes was plenty of movie.

These days, however, there are no newsreels, nor are there shorts and cartoons. And double features are unusual.

The typical film, therefore, standing alone in an evening's program, has grown longer. One hundred or one hundred ten minutes is about average. If the typical movie is a hundred minutes more or less, the typical screenplay is a hundred pages more or less.

Generally, all artists need to be economical; their challenge is to say a lot with a little. But a script that is less than a hundred pages begins to appear as if it might not fill an evening's program. And less than ninety pages is likely to be regarded as unprofessional.

A hundred and ten pages is about ideal; such a script seems substantial but not too long. A hundred and twenty pages is tolerable, but even that begins to appear bloated. When pages reach one-thirty plus, more often than not the script is out of hand and should be trimmed before being offered to agents and producers.

Compared to loftier considerations such as story, character, dialogue, or theme, all this talk about page-counts may seem trivial. But what is a screenplay if not pages? Far too many pages, or far too few, suggest a basic lack of soundness, an inability to understand the limits and requirements of the movie experience.

At UCLA I am an easy target for writers from outside

the university who besiege me daily with calls and letters pleading for a review of their screenplay. In fact I'm happy to oblige when I can. The first question I ask is: how many pages? One caller reports that his script is three hundred and forty pages; another says thirty-five. Such page-counts immediately clue any reader to the overwhelming likelihood the scripts are amateurish. No agent or producer will seriously consider any such screenplay.

Cruel as it may appear, aberrant page-count alone imparts to a script an aura of unprofessionalism. Of course, the proper number of pages cannot itself determine whether a script is any good; but all alone it can easily reveal the distinct probability it is bad.

A professional reader at a studio or agency who synopsizes and analyzes scripts most certainly prefers a screenplay of a hundred and five pages to one running a hundred-forty. Even before reading the short script he is its fan; of course, he may quickly change his mind, in some cases just as soon as he gets one third of the way down the first page.

But at least he starts out liking the script.

Conversely, the same reader hates the hundred-forty page script before he cracks page one. He sees such a screenplay as the barrier between himself and lunch. Indeed, writers can do a lot worse than to view their task simply as keeping the reader's mind off that pastrami sandwich awaiting him at the studio commissary.

A good writer makes his reader forget lunch.

There are exceptions. A friend and former student, writer/director Alex Cox (*Repo Man, Sid and Nancy, Straight to Hell, Walker*), in his earliest days at UCLA handed me a script running some hundred and seventy-nine pages. Before reading any of it, I lectured Alex professorially about the need for economy and efficiency not in film alone but in all creative expression. I pointed out to him that he was asking me to do his work for him, that he shouldn't hand a script of such length even to his teacher.

He pleaded that he had no idea where to cut the script.

I carried his screenplay around with me for perhaps two

weeks. Finally, on a day when I had meetings scheduled all around town, I planned to tackle it in fragments among the various appointments. But after the first meeting, upon reading the first several pages, I became so caught up in the script's intricate, spellbinding plot—quite uncharacteristic of the disjointed, quirky style for which Alex is now so widely celebrated—that I cancelled the rest of my meetings because I was that eager to find out what happened in this breathtaking tale.

And in the end I was in solid agreement with the writer that there was no earthly way to trim even a single scene from the script.

But any writer who bases his style and working methodology on such an anomalous example asks for trouble; he isolates himself from ninety-nine percent of agents and producers. Let such a script be his *second* project after he is the world-famous creator of a mega-hit and has acquired the clout to do whatever he chooses.

It is pertinent to note that at the present writing, ten years after the fact, and notwithstanding all of Alex's international acclaim, that hundred-seventy-nine page script remains unsold and unproduced.

Drafts

Every draft is a first draft.

Unless a script represents a commissioned assignment from a producer, studio, or network, in which a particular draft conforms to a specific contractual stipulation—say, that by a particular date a rewrite or polish is due—regardless of how many drafts and rewrites and polishes and repolishes, every script is the first draft.

This does not change the fact that when dealing in screenplays several drafts inevitably will be written. As discussed in the section on rewriting, no writer ever sits down without expecting to write the script flat-out perfect the first time. Of course it never happens. As surely as no pregnant woman expects to give birth to an adult, no writer should expect his first draft to emerge sufficiently mature as to be ready for agents and producers.

For once a draft is offered, no matter how kindly the reader reports his reaction, if it is negative he will not be interested in later drafts. The blush is off.

No matter how vast the selling price, virtually no first draft is filmed as is. This means that even if the draft is good enough to buy, there will still be changes to be made. Writers need, therefore, to learn how to say upon rejection: "Thank you for your consideration and attention." It's a self-defeating proposition to launch into paroxysms of: "I'm planning to change this and that; this is a metaphor for that, that is a metaphor for this. In this present draft I was really just sort of sketching out the basic ideas. May I ask you to take a second look when it's rewritten?"

If the script is going to be rewritten, it should have been rewritten *before* it was offered to readers. A reader has every right to ask: "If you plan to rewrite this, why'd you take up my time with it *now*?" He'll think twice before he reads another script by that particular writer.

Nowhere on a script, therefore, should there be any indication that a particular draft—even if it is the seventeenth—is anything besides the first. And the best way to abide by this rule is not to write First Draft or Rough Draft or First Rough Draft or Rough First Draft on the cover. Leave out draft numbers altogether.

Dates

Should a writer put the date of completion on his draft? No!

Again, this may not hold for a presold script written on assignment, in which a writer fulfills the precise stipulations of a contract. But in any other instance, unless he wants the script to grow old instantly, a writer should ignore the date.

Some writers believe that unless they put the little copyright squiggle accompanied by the year, the script is not legally protected. But, as discussed in Chapter 9, "Script

Sales Strategies," a screenplay is protected without formal copyright registration. What is more, and contrary to myth, plagiarism is simply not a problem in the movie business. Good characters, wonderful dialogue, compelling stories: *Those* are the problems.

A date on a draft simply dates it.

Notwithstanding the success of *Platoon*, a script that circulated for ten years before winning funds for production, there is in Hollywood an unspoken but clear prejudice against material that is not brand-new. Agents, producers, and their readers vastly prefer a new script to one that has made the rounds. Remember, even a script that is merely a few months old will be suspected of having traveled from producer to producer. And every writer wants every producer to think the script is being offered to him before anybody else in the universe. Why would a writer want to announce to prospective producers that others have already declined the opportunity to acquire his screenplay?

So unless you want your script to age right before your eyes—and the eyes of the entire film and television community—put no date on it.

Scenes

Should a writer number his screenplay's scenes?
Again, no.

This advice may seem confusing to new writers who have located existing scripts to read, as in so many the scenes are clearly numbered. But I reiterate, the draft of a published script, or one discovered in a library, a book shop, or located through a script service may not be the master-scene but the shooting script.

If writing a good screenplay is enormously difficult, numbering the scenes is easy; a secretary can do it after the script's written. I suspect the reason so many novice writers number their scenes is the same reason they include angles, lenses, close-ups, zooms—they believe it lends their script an aura of professionalism.

The sad irony is, of course, that precisely the opposite is accomplished; their script is made to appear amateurish.

Cover

Script reproduction services frequently offer the purchaser of as few as ten copies free laminated silver-flecked leatherette covers plus gold or black embossed press-on lettering.

Turn them down!

Try to see if the shop will instead toss in an extra copy or two; I hasten to volunteer that in my own experience I've never succeeded in winning this concession from any copier.

No matter; a fancy cover looks bad. And illustrated covers are worse. It's what lies between the covers that counts.

Years ago, working on a project in New York, represented by the veteran agent Knox Burger, I wondered aloud whether a particular draft was in acceptable physical shape to submit to my producer. "It should look like a writer wrote it," Knox responded.

A draft of a screenplay should look like a draft of a screenplay. It should be legible, properly formatted, and not more than that. Most certainly it should not look like an item from a vanity press, a self-published document intended for mass distribution as literature. Too elaborate a cover all by itself suggests the writer is not confident of his script's content.

What should appear on the cover? Two things: title, author.

I have already urged writers to leave out any information regarding dates and drafts. I urge them now further to exclude all information regarding Writers Guild registration. Please do not misunderstand: I most definitely recommend registering the script with the Guild. (Please see Chapter 9 for the proper procedure.) But that does not mean there is any reason in the world to say on the cover that the script is registered. Producers will assume that the script is registered. Expressing the fact on a script's cover and, as so many writers do, also including the registration number, suggests the writer is inexperienced and the script bush-league.

The writer of an original screenplay need not assert its originality on the cover page or anywhere else in the script. Writers do not, for that matter, need to say that their script is a screenplay at all. A reader sees it's a screenplay—it's got description, dialogue. What purpose in printing beneath the title "an original screenplay by"? If the writer does not say it is a screenplay, will the reader think it's a chicken salad sandwich?

Economy counts, therefore, even on a screenplay's cover. Subliminally, a cluttered cover page, with date, draft, registration numbers, and the writer's address and phone number(s), constitutes inefficiency. There is something wonderfully pristine and pure about a clean page with but title and author.

I say only title and author. I do not say title followed by the legend "written by" or even "by." If there is a title with a name beneath it, won't the reader figure that the name belongs to the writer?

Again, all by themselves, these precepts may not appear to carry a lot of weight. Collectively, however, they add up to an overall impression of a script that is desirable or not. All by themselves, they set the tone. And like so many other aspects of screenplay format, if there are limits to how much help they can provide a script, there are far fewer limits to how badly ignoring them can hurt one.

Here follow two examples of title pages: a good one and a bad one.

BOTTOM DOLLAR
Ike Warshaw

<u>"THE VILLAGE OF THE HAPPY NICE PEOPLE"</u>
an original screenplay written by
Ike Warshaw

(c. 1982—Ike Warshaw)

Fourth Rough Draft Revised
July 11, 1982

Ike Warshaw
1234567 E. Buffalo Speedway
Third Floor—Apartment # 314
Houston, Texas 56789

home phone (555) 555-5555
work phone (555) 555-5555
mother's phone (555) 555-5555

Registered, Writers Guild
of America, West, Inc.,
registration #5555555

Binding

I apologize to no one for discussing matters so seemingly mundane as a screenplay's proper binding. A correctly bound script may lack all quality, but an unconventionally bound script immediately suggests amateurishness to readers.

A properly bound screenplay utilizes brass brads, those round-headed fasteners with two flat tails, one slightly longer than the other. Push each of two brads through the holes drilled through the script, and spread them apart at the other end.

And that's all there is to that.

As with so many other aspects pertinent to screenwriting, what is significant about bindings is not so much what to do as what not to do. Virtually any other style of binding is a hint that the writer is inexperienced. Screenwriting is, after all, a matter of how one comes across, the impression one makes.

And what kind of impression is made upon a reader who, even before viewing the first word on the first page, realizes the script is unwieldy even in the physical sense, that it's a challenge just to hold it in his hands, the pages difficult to turn?

A producer told me that if she had two scripts to read but time enough for only one, and if one of those scripts had three brads and the other two, she would read the one with two brads. Convention maintains that two holes, not three, represents the professional standard. Is this petty? Even *I* think so; yet the point is worth repeating: There is no aspect of a script—not its typeface, not the chemical composition of its cover material, not its binding—that is truly separate from its overall soundness or lack thereof.

A writer of talent and discipline who takes the trouble to construct a strong story with good characters speaking dialogue worth hearing is not likely to print the script carelessly, to splatter its cover with distracting details, to bind it in a curious, off-putting fashion.

Title

Never underestimate the importance of a screenplay's title.

There are those who maintain that if you don't have the title of your script before you start writing, you're not ready to start writing. I'm sympathetic with this notion, but I'm also convinced it takes the principle just a mite too far.

Still, the point is important. A proper title testifies to the writer's focus, to the overall cohesion of the myriad elements constituting an integrated screenplay. Sometimes a writer may be ready to start writing without yet having found a title; he may discover the title within the work itself, perhaps in a good line of dialogue.

The best titles are abrupt, teasing, and somehow manage in the broadest sense to summarize the script. *Patton* tells it all. *Kramer vs. Kramer* resonates with the toe-to-toe, eyeball-to-eyeball conflict that lies at the story's heart.

About Last Night is a terrible title for a pretty fair film. It is no surprise that the original title was quite different: *Sexual Perversity in Chicago*. Because too many newspapers refused to print the latter—a sorry commentary on American journalism—the studio was forced at the last minute to change it and, indeed, the haste shows. The film enjoyed good business, but who can say how much more success it might have known under a better title?

A good title has to fit neatly on a marquee. A good title needs to fit neatly into the open-ended sentence: "Hey, let's go see . . ."

This suggests that a title must not be spread out all over the place, not only in the marquee sense, but also emotionally and intellectually. As with so many other aspects of screenplay format, a good title is no substitute for pale characters residing within a frail story. And again, as with the bulk of format questions, it's more a matter of harm avoided than quality added.

There's no magic to inventing a good title; or perhaps

there's nothing *but* magic. It's mainly a question of darting about, trying this one, that one, and seeing how each feels, determining from the sound whether it fits. The best titles are more likely to be discovered than invented. It's as if they're already there, hovering, waiting to be plucked from the air.

No Character or Cast Lists

A list of roles at the beginning of a screenplay is a sure sign the writer is unfamiliar with the form. Even worse are casting suggestions. Though a list of characters is appropriate to a play, even in a play it is no substitute for character development through incident and dialogue.

No actor appreciates such "help" in getting to know a character. He expects the character to be defined by the action and sound in the script. The proper place for character description is that point at which we first meet the character in the script, exactly as the audience will meet him on screen. And even then the description must be concise.

Effects—Fades, Cuts, Dissolves

In keeping with the principle that scripts should never be unnecessarily complicated, writers should leave optical effects out of their scripts just as they should exclude superfluous sound effects. The test, as always, is integration. If the effect is genuinely needed, if some identifiable, plot-enhancing, character-expanding facet is lost or blurred without the effect, the writer may include it in his script.

Otherwise he should leave it out.

Should writers write CUT TO: between scenes?

No.

What in the world does CUT TO add to a script besides words and, collectively, whole pages? I have read screenplays where if the CUT TO's were deleted, the script would shrink by ten pages.

If one scene follows another, and there is no CUT TO between them, will the reader expect the writer intended a ripple dissolve in which the image shimmers, blurs, and appears to be submerged in liquid? Will the reader expect that the intent was for a spiral wipe, a spinning headline effects whirling at the same time as it flies out toward the audience?

Of course not. If no effect is indicated between scenes, the reader will assume the leading scene cuts to that which follows.

I often read scripts replete not only with CUT TO's but even with HARD CUT TO's or SMASH CUT TO's. What in the world is a SMASH CUT? Writers tell me it's an abrupt, stark, intentionally jarring transfer from one scene to the next. But what is harder, faster, more abrupt, more jarring, more smashing than a plain old garden variety cut? The final frame at the tail of the previous scene is butt-spliced to the first frame at the head of the next. Is that not as hard as a cut can be?

There is an exception, however, to my plea to exclude CUT TO's. From time to time without a script, after an integrated sequence of scenes in a single segment of time and locale, when the tale moves to a new time, a new place, it can be helpful to provide a CUT TO in order to separate the end of one broad section from the next. It is a gentle way of saying: We're done with this business in this time and place; now we move to new business in a new time and place.

Remember, even fine scripts make relatively hard reading; readers need all the help they can get.

Fades and dissolves are as self-explanatory as cuts. A FADE-IN finds a scene slowly composing itself on the screen, usually from darkness, although it is possible also to fade in from bright, pure, linen white. And a DISSOLVE is an overlapping fade; one scene fades out at the same time as another fades in.

On those rare occasions when there *is* sufficient justification to warrant indicating an effect, that effect is written entirely in upper-case letters.

Traditionally a dissolve, as opposed to a cut, indicates time has passed between shots. Cuts, on the other hand, suggest one moment follows directly upon another. This was the case during film's classical period. These days, with audiences evermore familiar with film grammar, dissolves are rarely necessary. Generally these and all effects are esthetic choices best left to the editor.

Fades, in or out, in the current film era are as unnecessary as dissolves. From time to time, instead of cutting, it may be pleasing to fade in and out between scenes, but these are judgments best left to the writer's collaborators—the director and the editor.

Film characteristics that early audiences found terribly disruptive are nowadays perfectly acceptable. This is true even for jump cuts within scenes, when a piece of action seems almost to be missing.

Plainly stated, audiences today need a lot less information than they used to. They seem able to follow a tale's drift more effectively than in earlier times.

I expect this is due largely to decades of exposure to television. Pundits love to denigrate television's influence, the numbing, bludgeoning effect of so much information sprayed upon so many people for so much time. But television has also helped people learn to absorb scattered information far more quickly than ever before. The typical television hour involves teasers, trailers (coming attractions), and commercials, each a separate show in itself, however brief, complete with its own beginning, middle, and end. There are also billboards for the upcoming news ("film at eleven") and announcements regarding future programs, plus bits of programs, constantly interrupted by still more sets of planned, orchestrated interruptions. Say what you will about TV's relentless blizzard of data; it has prepared audiences to follow stories that would have been confusing to earlier generations of viewers.

Screenwriters need to provide fewer technical indications, therefore, in order to help audiences limp along a movie's connective tissue. They need supply merely a fabulous story, sensitive characters, and startlingly clever, incisive dialogue.

P.O.V.

P.O.V. stands for Point of View. When included in a shot as follows:

EXT   THE ROAD   HARRY'S P.O.V.

it means that the audience views the road from precisely the same perspective as Harry; it is as if the lens is Harry's eye.

The telephoto binocular-matted shot of what a man sees, following the image of the man peering through binoculars, is an all too familiar example of a P.O.V. shot.

A Raymond Chandler story, *Lady in the Lake,* was made into a film that was one hundred percent P.O.V., as if viewed perpetually from one person's vantage as represented by the camera. Predictably, overuse of any effect quickly becomes gimmicky. And *Lady in the Lake,* while fun at first, quickly grows tedious.

A note of caution: Be certain to avoid using P.O.V. when intending simply to describe the image on screen. I once read a student's script in which a character was to sit in a chair.

The shot called for: RAYMOND   P.O.V. CHAIR.

It is amusing to contemplate what this shot would have looked like on screen had the writer's instructions been followed. There would have been, of course, a big bottom descending toward the lens, as if Raymond were being viewed by the chair!

Avoid "We See" and "We Hear"

As already indicated, the stuff in the wide margins—description, action, business—is information intended to be communicated visually. That within the narrower margins—for the most part dialogue—is to be communicated via the sound track. For writers to specify "we see" or "we hear," therefore, is simply redundant. In a properly formatted script it ought to be clear precisely which is which.

In the case of sound effects, these need merely to be capitalized within the scene description. For example: There is the SOUND of a car's ENGINE STARTING. What purpose is served by saying "we hear"?

Such rules may appear trivial, and perhaps all by themselves they truly are. But in screenplays they do not appear by themselves. Violations collectively nibble away at a script's edge and hint at the writer's inexperience.

Present Tense Only

Quest for Fire is a film set tens of thousands of years in the past; *Star Wars* takes place in the distant future. But both films play upon the screen now, today, this very minute.

That's why screenwriters should tell their stories in the present tense regardless of the script's setting in time. As soon as a reader reads that something "happened" or "occurred," he appreciates the writer is not conversant with film's basic nature.

Some years ago a student in an advanced screenwriting class wrote a script involving terrorists who, at tale's opening, seize, blindfold, and abduct a journalist. There follows a host of other scenes involving other characters in scattered locales. Then, at last, we meet up again with the hostage and his captors in their lair.

The script at this point notes that the victim's "blindfold has been removed."

I chastised (ever so gently) the writer for using the past tense "has been," and insisted (more gently still) he say simply that the blindfold "is removed."

The writer hesitated. Wouldn't that suggest that the audience sees the blindfold actively being removed, even though this is not the writer's intent?

But, I inquired, isn't that to be preferred? Instead of starting off the scene with the blindfold already gone, why not open with the blindfold actively being removed? Doesn't that more effectively connect the scene to the earlier one? And doesn't that render the script more active, less passive, and does that not make for a finer movie?

Thinking this way spurred the student to conceive yet another idea. Why not show it from the prisoner's P.O.V.? That is, at scene's opening have the blindfold cover the camera lens and, as it is removed, the audience is provided a sense of the scene from the character's own perspective.

My view was that this takes the notion a trifle too far, lending the scene unnecessary clutter. But it is significant that from a petty prescription to tell movie tales in the present tense, there arose a flurry of creative thinking, precisely the sort of mental process that makes for more inventive, imaginative film stories. Attention to even the most technical little screenwriting format rule can open up a broad vantage on creativity.

Theatrical Films Versus Movies for Television

There is no shortage of commentators asserting that certain kinds of screenplays are especially suited for theaters while others perfectly fit television.

Respectfully, this is just so much hogwash.

These same people would have sworn that a brawling, sprawling biblical epoch on the order of *Masada*, for example, could work only on the broad canvas of a football-field-sized screen in a movie palace. In fact, of course, *Masada* proved most effective on tiny, tidy television, where it found its vast and faithful audience.

They also would have you believe that a close-focus, personal, emotional family drama along the lines of, say, *Kramer vs. Kramer* or *Terms of Endearment,* would work only on television. And again they would be wrong; both play exceptionally well on the big screen.

It is worth remembering, therefore, that there are but two kinds of movies. And these are not television movies and theatrical movies.

They are good movies and bad movies.

As noted elsewhere in this volume, every pseudo-intellectual believes he can secure his perch among the elite by "discovering" that television is mediocre. But this is rank snobbism. In fact, television is more like other forms of creative expression than it is different from them. Most of it fails; some small portion of it is splendid.

The last thing I would do, therefore, is to attempt to dissuade screenwriters from writing movies for television. But I strenuously urge these same writers to avoid indicating anywhere within their script that the project is intended for TV.

This may seem to be a contradiction, but it is not. From the standpoint of a writer submitting material to an agent or a producer there isn't any useful reason to differentiate between theater and television. Both the theatrical feature and the m.o.w. (TV movie of the week), absent commercials, run approximately the same number of minutes and pages. A reader considering a project apparently intended for the big screen can just as easily view it as something suited for television.

More important, thanks to elitism's prevalence, writers are wise to avoid stating via format that their script is intended for television. To do so unnecessarily constricts the already limited vision of too many potential representatives and purchasers. Given the ingrained prejudice against TV, even among executives and agents who themselves service the television industry, people will be put off by contemplating that a concept was originated with "mere" television in mind.

Happily enough, the reverse prejudice does not obtain. That is to say, a script apparently written for theatrical release can be easily considered as an m.o.w. Therein lies all the reason required for a writer to avoid specifying one or the other. Let the reader think it's a theatrical feature. If it finds favor as a television film, it is easy enough after the fact to insert those quirks of format—an opening teaser plus seven separate commercial breaks—that identify it as such.

Spelling (and Punctuation) Count(s)!

Language is all that is available for writers to convey their fantasies, to ply their trade. There is nothing the least bit trivial, therefore, about punctuation, grammar, and spelling. If writers don't nurture and protect language, who will?

Typographical errors, rotten spelling, lousy punctuation, and sloppy grammar attest all too clearly to carelessness and imprecision, mortal enemies of good writing. I never see a script with a fabulous story and worthy characters speaking brilliant dialogue that also just happens to contain bad spelling, punctuation, grammar, and format. These items are all a measure of the dedication that goes—or does not go—into the writing. A good writer does not expend the effort necessary to weave memorable characters and story and at the same time pay positively no heed to language.

Screenwriting is a function of appreciating how one comes across. The successful artist understands the impression he makes. Clearly, a writer who cares not a whit about how he translates is not likely to make a desirable impression.

If he can't get the easy stuff, how will he get the hard?

A confession: I am myself the world's worst speller! Yet my scripts are (damned near) perfectly spelled.

How can this be? My computer's spell-check program?

In fact I avoid spell-correcting software altogether. (See the section on word processing in Chapter 8.) I still plow through the dictionary constantly, seeking correct spellings and, tangentially, delighting in all the discoveries I make while doing so. There are some words—*occurrence, necessarily*—that I look up every single time! But I am just plain ashamed to hand in a professional writing assignment that is misspelled.

Flashback

Movie cliches, like all cliches, become cliches in no small part because they are so useful.

If a writer wishes to utilize a flashback to help tell his tale, he should first decide that it is the best, most efficient, most articulate way of making his point. For the sorry fact is that the flashback, like the voice-over narration, is a much abused screenwriting conceit.

Still, it has its place.

Ideally, once the decision has been made to use a flashback, it should be integrated into the format exactly as it will be absorbed by the audience viewing it on screen. In the golden olden days, flashbacks used to start with rippling shimmer-dissolves, as if to clue the audience that we are now seeping, slipping, bleeding our way backward in time. But with today's movie-literate audiences, such devices are no longer necessary.

Ideally, again, the flashback should occur in the script exactly as it will appear on screen. If it takes some measure of time for the audience to realize we have moved into the past, such uncertainty can be exploited by the writer as a tension-creating device.

The effect may be clearer on screen, however, than on

the page; the filmed, visual information is so much more lush than the black-and-white of the written script. Upon calling the shot or within the context of the shot itself, writers may want explicitly to indicate that the current action is a flashback.

Such a shot might read:

EXT   THE BARN — FLASHBACK

The point, as always, is to help the reader follow the story as it will be followed on screen.

Cheating

In a screenplay, to label a flashback as a flashback represents a kind of cheat. After all, in the purest sense, it ought to become clear within the story that a certain sequence is a flashback. The writing should articulate that information. Draping little clues on the page, indicating "flashback," and attaching hints to the screen such as optical effects like a ripple dissolve, are heavy-handed methods for spoonfeeding readers and audiences. If the audience in the theater can live without the opticals, as these days they generally can, cannot also the reader of a script be left to figure out for himself that a flashback is a flashback?

The problem is, of course, that the screen provides information so much more abundantly than the page. The reader sometimes needs a bit of help. In movies this kind of help is often characterized as a "cheat.' And if in life to cheat is immoral and unethical, in films it is perfectly acceptable. Films are in their essence, after all, from start to finish not much more than elaborate cheats.

Sometimes, therefore, in helping the reader to follow the tale as written on the page, here and there a writer may wisely offer a bit of a cheat. He may say for example that a particular character "remembers" something or "realizes" something else. He may spell out for the reader that a flashback is a flashback. He may even specify a hint of action to come, even though this technically contradicts the most basic tenet of screenwriting format.

This manner of cheating is useful as long as it is not abused, for writers who cheat too broadly, too frequently, take readers for something they are not: fools. In such instances writers fool only themselves.

Writers who cheat successfully, therefore, transcend mere sight and sound by violating one of screenwriting's fundamental rules. Nevertheless, it is a perfectly acceptable technique for achieving clarity in screenplays. The key is to cheat with consummate skill and to do so most sparingly.

Cheating is a phenomenon that occurs not only on the page but on the stage—the soundstage—as well. A director will instruct an actor to "cheat" his look—focus his attention not on the face of the person to whom he speaks but to a spot several degrees east or west of there, as on camera it may more effectively fulfill editorial requirements.

Movies, ultimately, along with all artistic expression, should uncover the basic truths underlying the essential nature of man, woman, and universe. Ironically, one way in which they fulfill this holy calling is to cheat like crazy.

Gentle Reminders for Readers

One useful screenwriting cheat is to offer the reader little reminders from time to time of what he has already read.

This is cheating because, ideally, the information in the script should unfold precisely as it will on screen. Difficulty derives, however, from the fact that the images projected upon the screen, combined with the actual sound track, provide far richer data. A character on the page, for example, is just ink—not much more than a name plus the briefest description. On screen, however, that same character, even before he speaks, even before he takes any action, may be instantaneously recognizable as a world-famous movie star. Clint Eastwood is Clint Eastwood; Jane Fonda is Jane Fonda. Should they appear briefly, then reappear later, nobody needs to be reminded as to their identity.

On the page, however, the reader may very well need some assistance. Even an unknown actor provides more information to the theater audience than his part, seen in the script, offers the reader. An actress, even a complete unknown, on screen possesses a certain look, speaks in a particular voice, stands with a specific slouch. Should she appear briefly in an early scene, and then reappear much later, the audience has a far better chance of remembering her than does the reader, for whom she was merely a collection of inky squiggles expressed as words on the page.

This is why it is justifiable now and again to remind the reader who is who and what is what. For example: "Jenny, the woman seen earlier driving the car . . ." If technically this is a violation, in the interest of readability such gentle reminders are advisable.

Montage

Montage, like flashback, has long ago become something of a film cliche. But again, if overuse has hurt it, the reason it is used so much is that it frequently proves useful as an economical way of quickly exposing a great deal of required information.

At the same time, however, montage is too often used to pad and pump a film that lacks sufficient weight. In the otherwise charming *Elvira Madigan,* for example, there is a host of montages in which the young lovers float slow-motion through fields of flowers, with Mozart playing lushly in the background all the while. Pretty as it is, it quickly becomes quite boring, since it lacks all sense of story and character development and advances the film's thrust not a bit. Instead of serving as an economizing device, therefore, it provides the opposite effect.

Screenwriters considering montage should decide first of all to avoid it where at all possible. Second, they should use it as an efficiency-making device in the depicting of complicated sequences.

A chase is a typical example. The opening of *Beverly Hills Cop* contains a startling race through Detroit streets in which big-rig trailers chase each other and are themselves chased by police cars. Described shot for shot, such a sequence might occupy several pages of script.

But if viewing such a chase on screen is any fun, reading about it in a script is not. The reader wants to know the essential action and plot points. What is the basic nature of the chase? Does the prey escape or is he apprehended?

In such an instance, instead of describing this shot and that one, the trucks, the police cars, the writer is best off simply calling the shot CHASE, and then listing the salient features as they arise. In this manner a lot of pages are saved, as well as a lot of the reader's time.

Years ago I read the first draft of a comedy in which the cops chase not a truck but a paisley-emblazoned hippie-style souped-up school bus. The writer called virtually every shot. In the second draft he reduced it to a far simpler montage:

EXT ROADS AND HIGHWAYS — THE CHASE

POLICE CARS with lights flashing and SIRENS SCREAMING pursue the speeding BUS.

— the bus departs the main road;
— a police car, following, runs into a ditch;
— a second police car crashes into the one in front of it;
— the bus sails off safely into the sunset.

In this fashion an unwieldy, marginally readable thirteen pages of chase were reduced to one-fifth of a page.

Upper Case and Lower

How does a screenwriter decide which names and terms to capitalize within a screenplay?

There are various well-established rules. As each character is introduced for the first time in the screenplay, his name should be entirely upper case. And whenever his name appears above a line of his dialogue, again, caps all the way. In my view, a character's name should also be capitalized the first time he is introduced into every scene in which he appears. This way a reader scanning the page is immediately cognizant of the scene's characters.

It makes for easier reading. And easier reading is a major reason we bother with format in the first place.

But there is another reason for format. And while it seems to be highly technical, it is enormously purposeful for writers, too. It involves the production manager.

The way format came to evolve as it has is so that a production manager can turn a script into a nuts-and-bolts production plan. He needs to break down a movie in terms of budget, in terms of actors, actresses, props, costumes, essential sound effects, and all the other countless details that constitute a film.

That's why, for example, integrated sound effects are also written upper case. If, for example, a GUNSHOT is indicated in a scene, the production manager will need to alert the sound editor to create that cue or to locate it in a sound-effects library. Placing it in caps, therefore, is a way of making sure he sees all the details for which he needs to make arrangements.

We write, of course, not for production managers but for readers. Still, the same rules apply. The subtle nuances of image and sound come fully to exist only when the film is finally shot and edited. Prior to that, in order to provide the reader a thorough understanding of the imagined film, it is helpful to get those same salient facts to stand out from the general descriptions. Upper-case letters accomplish that.

A reader scans a scene and quickly sees which characters are in it, as well as the important props and necessary sound effects, all of which, if truly integrated, no doubt go a long way toward explaining the essential action. And if there are important, integrated, character-advancing, plot-advancing sound effects, these are indicated in capital letters, not simply because it's easier for the production manager to spot them, but because the reader can see them too.

Sloppy format not only makes it difficult for a production manager to determine what is concretely needed, it makes an amateurish impression on readers. It makes it difficult for readers to figure out the who, what, where, when, and why of a screenplay. It makes it unlikely that a screenplay will ever get as far as a production manager's office.

There is plenty of leeway within different format approaches. Writers should read as many scripts as they can so as to see the various techniques. And then they should choose their own style, integrating techniques that appeal to them and seem to promise to help them tell their tale in the clearest manner possible.

I close this chapter on format by presenting an example of standard American screenplay format. Please note that "INT" stands for "interior" and signifies a scene set indoors; similarly, "EXT" means "exterior" and denotes a scene set outdoors.

Note Tab Settings:

#1 business

#2 dialogue

#3 parentheticals

#4 character's
   name

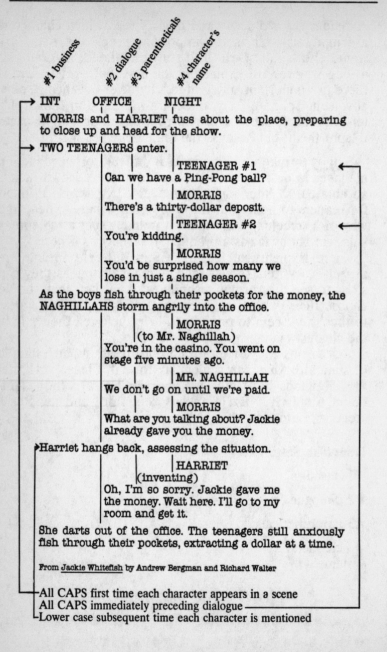

#1 business   #2 dialogue   #3 parentheticals   #4 character's name

INT   OFFICE   NIGHT

MORRIS and HARRIET fuss about the place, preparing to close up and head for the show.

TWO TEENAGERS enter.

                    TEENAGER #1
          Can we have a Ping-Pong ball?

                    MORRIS
          There's a thirty-dollar deposit.

                    TEENAGER #2
          You're kidding.

                    MORRIS
          You'd be surprised how many we
          lose in just a single season.

As the boys fish through their pockets for the money, the NAGHILLAHS storm angrily into the office.

                    MORRIS
                 (to Mr. Naghillah)
          You're in the casino. You went on
          stage five minutes ago.

                    MR. NAGHILLAH
          We don't go on until we're paid.

                    MORRIS
          What are you talking about? Jackie
          already gave you the money.

Harriet hangs back, assessing the situation.

                    HARRIET
                 (inventing)
          Oh, I'm so sorry. Jackie gave me
          the money. Wait here. I'll go to my
          room and get it.

She darts out of the office. The teenagers still anxiously fish through their pockets, extracting a dollar at a time.

From Jackie Whitefish by Andrew Bergman and Richard Walter

All CAPS first time each character appears in a scene
All CAPS immediately preceding dialogue
Lower case subsequent time each character is mentioned

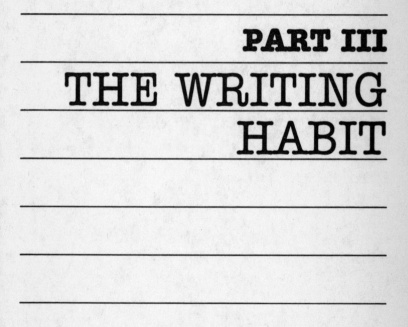

PART III
THE WRITING HABIT

8

Writer's Block

and Tackle

When asked to offer his single most important piece of advice for writers, writer Tommy Thompson responded after a long, thoughtful pause: Every day, no matter what else you do, get dressed. The most destructive mistake a writer can make, Thompson insisted, is to sit around the house all day in his bathrobe.

Thompson did not talk about inspiration. He did not mention grammar and spelling. Neither did he say anything about research techniques, or character, dialogue, or plot. And this was not because he considered these items unimportant. Rather, he understood that none of these counts at all if writers don't first master something else: the writing habit.

As emphasized in Chapter 10, writers are for the most part a fussy, finicky lot. And as asserted in the Introduction, not one of them truly likes to write.

It is not fair, therefore, to expect writers ever to want to write. Instead, they simply must write. For better or worse—actually for a bit of both—writing must become an ingrained, routinized procedure that simply cannot be shaken except by further writing. For without the writing habit, a firm grip on story structure, a thorough understanding of characterization, a brilliant ear for dialogue, and a crafty sense of business savvy all add up to nothing.

Ideas

Among writing's most overrated quantities is the idea.

I have never met soul who did not have a fabulous idea for a movie. Worse, people seem forever eager to share these ideas with writers. But working writers don't need other people's ideas; they ought to have plenty of their own. For ideas, even the best among them, are still merely ideas. All by themselves they are cheap. What has genuine value is the idea that is worked out and written down, structured into a story with characters speaking nifty dialogue, a tale meriting and sustaining an audience's attention for a hundred minutes.

The problem for a writer about to commence an original screenplay is not to find an idea but to discard all the other ideas he already has, arriving at that one to which he is willing to commit hundreds of hours struggling.

Ideas occur in odd places and at curious moments. A writer sees a flash of action in real life; it may be grandiose and spectacular—a house ablaze—but more likely it is mundane: a depositor quarreling with a bank teller, a nun at roadside changing a tire.

Whatever it is, the writer may find himself from time to time involuntarily thinking about the incident or the idea. He may discover that it reminds him of something in his own life. He may attach fictional incidents and anecdotes. Soon, but not *too* soon, he may begin to sense a three-act structure asserting itself.

E. L. Doctorow describes in an interview how he invented *Ragtime*. In a full-bore writer's depression, a total famine of ideas, not a clue as to what he might write about, he began pacing around his study in his home in New Rochelle, New York. After a long while he found himself pressing his face in despair against the wall, and so finally he started to write about the wall. He imagined the wall today, and the house to which it belongs, and then he worked his way back to when the house was built early in the century, and soon he was writing about New Rochelle at the turn of the century, and weaving an imaginative tale involving leading personalities and colorful events of that era. And before he knew what was happening, he was writing *Ragtime.*

With regard to original screenplays, many writers finally sit down to write a script once the idea has quietly percolated for a year or more.

Almost any idea, even a bad one, can be turned into a good screenplay. Indeed, when I was just starting out as a screenwriter, while still enrolled as a student at the University of Southern California film school, I was now and again approached by producers who had ideas and sought to hire writers to turn them into screenplays. In such instances my greatest struggle was to remember not to tell the producer how terrific I thought the idea until he actually *told* it to me.

As a starving student/fledgling writer I was not about to tell any producer eager to spend thousands of dollars on an unknown writer that his idea did not interest me. I admit now that sometimes I accepted ideas that I regarded poorly, or at least feigned more enthusiasm than I actually felt. And from some fairly spongy ideas I was able to create solid screenplays satisfying not only my employers but even myself.

An idea is just an idea. If it's good, all that remains is the work, the invention, the integration, the characterizations, the settings, dialogue—in short, the writing.

Writer's Block

Once a writer has played with an idea in his mind for many months, he may decide it is time actually to put pencil to paper. But he may also find that he is stuck, that he just can't seem to get started. Or a writer may be well into a script that has been flowing smoothly for many pages only to become stuck.

A writer who truly wants to start writing must first of all shed the naive need to enjoy himself. Enjoyment is for audiences. Enjoyment is for later. Fun is for *after* writing.

Blocked writers who sit around idly waiting for inspiration, hoping against hope for some probing insight, are forever condemned to stagnation and self-contempt. The cure? Simply start writing. Never mind good, bad, indifferent. Just get words onto paper. And if a day passes with the writer stumbling clumsily through even only two, three, or four pages, and if out of all that there is but a page, or a page plus a fragment of another page, that is even remotely useful, a writer could at such a pace—even taking weekends off—write three to four respectable screenplays every year.

To put it bluntly, writer's block is a hoax. Blockage is writing's natural state. It derives from the immature notion that writing ought to be fun, ought to be easy, ought to flow like Niagara, or if not quite Niagara, like some dependable country creek.

Over the years, working writers have suggested a broad menu of techniques to deal with writer's block—change locales, change working hours, switch from typewriter to felt-tipped markers. But the only certain remedy for writer's block is writing. The blocked writer's salvation lies in learning not to shun but to embrace the inevitable reluctance that accompanies all creative activity.

When new writers complain to me that they are frustrated, I tell them I am actually glad to hear it because it signals to me that they are having the sorts of real experiences belonging to real writers.

No writer has a right to expect to *want* to write. To dissolve the obstruction in his creativity a writer need merely plant his rear in his chair and his fingers on his keys—and keep it/them there for several hours each day.

Working Methods

Writing, solitary enterprise that it is, requires writers to find their own individual methods, to create their own daily schedule and routine.

When I was just starting out, I looked outside myself to other writers for cues as to the right and the wrong of it. Two of my USC film school classmates had already become quite a successful team, and for too many years I criticized myself for failing to follow the schedule they devised for themselves. They were at the writing table by eight, worked without pause until precisely twelve-thirty, took off exactly thirty minutes for lunch—always the same lunch: tuna fish, no mayonnaise, just a splash of lemon juice—then worked again all afternoon, no nonsense tolerated, writing until five-thirty.

As senility and decrepitude encroach ever more closely upon me, I now more readily surrender to my own quirks and instincts. Intellectually, I should prefer to be able to rise bright and early, plant myself immediately by the warm, glowing screen of my faithful word processor, boot up the cruise control, write productively, indeed inspirationally until noon, or maybe even one-thirty, and call it quits for the day. Instead, I rarely get to the screen until one or two, and every bit as rarely start any actual writing until a couple of hours later, working into the early and middle evening hours.

That's the way it is for me, that's the way it's always been, and if past is prologue, for me that's the way it's going to be. After so many years working in such a fashion, I finally surrender to the routine, and at long last realize that this is my own natural rhythm and there's no useful purpose in resisting.

Writers need to permit themselves to achieve in whatever manner serves. Some work slowly, steadily, all day, day after day. Others dawdle hour after hour until, with hardly any time left at the end of each day, they leap suddenly into an orgy of finger-flailing productivity.

Other writers start in the evening and work all night. Still others work in their heads for months, putting nothing on paper, then lock themselves in a garage or cabin or motel and write endlessly, around the clock, catnapping here and there until their task is complete.

Some writers measure their output by hours, others by pages. For everything else writing is—story, language, inspiration, character, art, craft—first of all it is pages. When you get right down to it, there's page one, then comes two, which is followed by three, and all the rest after that. It may not be romantic to look upon it quite that way, but for working writers that's the way it truly is.

Writing habits and working methodologies are as personal and individual as writing itself, and each writer needs to find his own method, his own schedule, and not rely upon others to set some authorized standard. Instead of intellectualizing about how he ought to work, a writer should just work.

Writing Venue

Among the many myths about writing is that writers hate to be disturbed.

In truth, working writers *live* for disturbance. A writer who is not from time to time interrupted soon finds himself compiling lengthy shopping lists, cleaning his nails, rereading the lost-dog ads in the classified. Myself, I phone 800 numbers, tilting toward Utah ski reports.

The lost little cabin in the woods—no neighbors for miles, no disruption save the chirping of birds—is the novice's dream but the working writer's nightmare. In such a setting a real writer soon goes stark, raving mad.

A world-famous mathematician accomplishes his finest theoretical analyses in airport lounges. He goes to the airport even when he's not flying anywhere, just to sit and scratch out his notes and formulae on odd slips of paper balanced precariously on his lap. He finds the tense, swirling motion of displaced people all about him somehow calming. It is as if the anxiety and confusion requires him to concentrate.

In Los Angeles writers are easily isolated. We work alone in our studies, sometimes never leave the house for days or even weeks, travel alone in our cars, and all too rarely interact with drama's only true source: people.

This is one more reason I rejoice to be part of the greater UCLA community, where people move about on foot and actually talk to each other, exchanging wonderfully inconsequential small talk. The university setting provides a writer with a superstructure of support; it gives him a chance to practice such outlandish activities as greeting people. "Hello, how are you? Nice to see you. Myself? Just fine, thanks." That may not seem like a whole lot, but for writers, social cripples as we tend to be, it constitutes a thrilling union with humanity. Interestingly, I find some of my richest, most successful former students hiding in library carrels at UCLA even though they have fancy office suites at major studios, and luxurious seaside retreats at Malibu.

Must one live in Los Angeles or New York in order to ply the screenwriting trade?

Most definitely not.

As discussed in Chapter 9, "Script Sales Strategies," introductions to agents and producers are best achieved not by personal visits or even by telephone calls but by the United States Postal Service. Writers, especially inexperienced writers, are best off not attempting to win commissioned assignments verbally pitching ideas to producers, but by speculating on a feature-length screenplay, and then speculating on yet another.

A writer eager to work specifically in episodic television benefits by being located in Los Angeles, it is true, as this happens to be where the business is. But I also know writers who live far from town, send in their episodes direct from their computers via modem, and rarely—if regularly—visit the town to meet with producers and agents.

Where a writer writes counts less than what he writes.

Outline vs. Treatment

Prior to jumping in and writing, in order to create a script that is integrated, sustained, and worthy of an audience's consideration, a writer needs a plan.

One way to plan is to construct an outline.

Remember that an outline is not a treatment. Treatments, to my mind, are hardly worth treating since they are a form most writers dread. They tend to take the fun out of screenwriting. A treatment is simply a description of a movie, told, as with all screenplays, in the present tense. A treatment is an outline that has been fattened up and sanitized.

When writers submit a treatment accompanying a script that has already been written, the treatment is read instead of the script. If writers, especially new writers, submit treatments for scripts that have yet to be written, the agent or producer is not likely to give it much attention, as no matter how brilliant it may be, it still provides no solid proof that the writer can write a screenplay. In rare instances where unknown writers actually succeed in selling treatments, better-known writers are usually hired to write the screenplay.

Writers are best off forgetting treatments altogether and paying attention to screenplays. And again, before writing a screenplay, a writer needs to write an outline.

In many ways, it is harder to outline a screenplay than it is to write one, for if any part of writing can be said to be fun, it is that which follows the careful process of outlining. That's when the writer truly meets his characters for the first time, hears their dialogue, and is now and again surprised by the tricks they play on him. Moreover, each day as he writes his quota of pages and adds them to the pile, he derives immeasurable satisfaction from knowing soon he'll have a draft, something he can hold in his hand and thump against the desk. You can't thump an idea, a concept, a notion against any desk. Only pages will do.

To create a solid, useful outline, on the other hand, takes lots of time and results in precious few pages; the writer is denied the comforting vision of that ever-accumulating pile of pulp. The process itself is like trying to carry steam in a bucket; outlines are vaporous. Compared to scripting an actual draft, it's hard to get a handle on the elements. In outlines writers deal with wisps of actions, ghosts of characters, translucent ideas, intangible quantities.

And from these ethereal items they are required to fashion solid, shapely tales to entice, seduce, enthrall.

Is it any wonder outlining is among writing's most frustrating experiences?

But it is also among the most necessary.

A still-admired but largely burned-out playwright not long ago revealed that whereas early in his career he carefully, painstakingly wrote detailed outlines, more recently—presumably because he is now so vastly experienced—he just sits down and writes his plays from scratch. Tragically, his current works appear to be written precisely that way. They are scattered, haphazard, disjointed, disorganized; the playwright clearly cares not a lot about his plays, and neither do audiences.

Outlining is just what it implies, the construction of a broad overview of the story line, a list of scenes, a shapely catalogue of events, incidents, and anecdotes collectively constituting the tale's raw bones.

Outlines need as much detail as necessary so that the writer—nobody else—may fully know his tale. It is possible to become so preoccupied with detail that the outline becomes a substitute for the script itself. In such an instance a screenplay risks appearing mechanical, cold, aloof. It may all fit together neatly enough, but it will lack warmth and spirit.

The challenge of outlines is to fill them as richly as possible while at the same time leaving room for surprises. Outlines should contain little actual dialogue.

An outline ought to be a temporary guide. If in the midst

of writing the actual script a better idea visits itself upon the writer, he ought to seize it.

A point arrives during outlining at which the writer may feel he's *almost* ready; and when he feels that way, he probably *is* ready. In writing, as in life, there is no such state as completely, perfectly ready.

Scene Cards

A second technique for planning a screenplay involves the use of scene cards. Scene cards and outlines are not mutually exclusive methodologies; writers can usefully integrate the two.

A scene card is just what it says: an index card containing a number relating to its position within the sequence of scenes throughout the film, the setting of the particular scene, a notation as to the characters appearing in it, and a brief description—one or two sentences—of the action that transpires.

Many writers find scene cards far more useful, far easier to work with than the traditional outline with its numbered list of scenes. For one thing, with scene cards it's simpler to experiment, to switch scenes' order, to shuffle them around. Scene cards provide writers with a hands-on feel for their story.

Occasionally, a writer will know that a scene is needed in a particular place within a tale, but he may not be certain precisely how that scene should be mounted, what action it should contain, which characters ought to participate. With scene cards it's easy to sketch several such scenes and keep them handy until, in the broader context arrived at later, it becomes clear which scene serves best, and where precisely it may fit.

With scene cards, again, it's just that much easier to try things out, and trying things out is what screenwriting—especially tale assembly—is all about.

A typical movie contains perhaps sixty such scenes, although that depends upon what precisely the writer considers a scene to be. One writer's scene is another's sequence; one writer's sequence is another's shot. By my own estimation, a scene is a unified piece of action in a single setting with its own clear beginning, middle, and end. It can be as brief as in *The Godfather,* where the man wakes up to discover his prize racehorse's bloody head in his bed: asleep, awake, horror. Or it can be as complex as the finish to *The Bridge on the River Kwai,* where Alex Guinness looks proudly to his completed bridge, then to the abandoned dynamite plunger, then to the train clattering toward the overpass, and finally runs madly to the detonator upon which he falls, recovering his senses and destroying his own evil creation. Every scene in every well-written film is a mini-movie all by itself, with its own time frame and structure.

Scene cards are particularly handy in helping writers maintain an overall sense of their tale. A writer needs to be able to skip over this part and that one when he is not quite certain, and keep on moving forward in order to find the key plot points and other pivotal moments. He needs to be able to live with a certain uncertainty.

Scene cards enable the writer to accomplish this in the same way film editors assemble an incomplete film, one for which certain scenes have not yet returned from the lab. They utilize a technique called slugging, that is, inserting a blank piece of film into a missing scene's place until the actual footage is available.

Writers working with scene cards can similarly slug scenes; they can insert a blank card, or one with merely some superficial suggestions. In this way they can move forward without becoming bogged down in the infinite minutia at the heart of all filmmaking.

A useful method integrates both outlining and scene cards. A writer starts a script from a carefully constructed outline. Without preparing scene cards, he proceeds directly from the outline to write the first draft of the script. Then, upon running into trouble (as writers seem almost invariably to do around the end of the middle, approximately two thirds of the way through), he returns to the beginning of the script and spends a morning, or a day, scene-carding his tale *as if it did not exist.* That is to say, he creates scene cards from as much of the script as is already written. The physical manipulation, the reproduction of the story on crisp, firm cards, sometimes furnishes the momentum necessary to push the story's leading edge through the barrier that's got it blocked.

Rewriting

After all the planning, outlining, scene-carding, after a first draft is written, at long last it can be rewritten.

And after it has been rewritten it can be rewritten again. Real writing, and especially reel writing, *is* rewriting.

Notwithstanding the inevitable truth of this proposition, no writer ever sits down to start a new project without thinking to himself this time, at long last, I'm going to get it all perfectly right the first time. I may go a little more slowly, I may move forward with just a tad more deliberation, but what I write will stay written exactly as it is written.

But this is never, ever the case.

Sometimes a student tells me he's keenly resistant to the process of outlining, that he prefers instead to write an unplanned, oversized, rambling, rumbling, overblown first draft. He admits he's not sure precisely how the tale will unravel, but cannot figure out any other way to get into it than to get into it. If he feels strongly enough about it, notwithstanding my warning to the contrary, I encourage him to get started. If all he gets out of the experience is a sprawling, brawling, unwieldy, all-over-the-place rough draft, he can use that draft as his outline and eventually sculpt the tale into shapely, appealing form through massive rewriting.

Whatever a writer's eccentricities, there is no escape from the need to rewrite. No matter what techniques a writer employs, eventually he ends up rewriting. Rewriting is so integral to writing's nature that writers can find themselves rewriting their picture in their minds years after it has been filmed, distributed, and exhibited. So it is possible, therefore, to rewrite too much. A script can be written over and over until the life has been written out of it. More often than not, I suspect, this kind of manic rewriting derives from a writer's reluctance to let go of his tale. For one thing, no one will criticize a script until the writer actually finishes it and gives it to somebody to read. Eventually a writer has to decide to take a stand: The time has come for me to show this sucker to people.

More narrowly, and every bit as problematic, is the tendency among many writers to rewrite each day's pages from the very beginning. This can cause the front end of a script to become slick and brassy, as the back end, instead of getting closer, seems to grow increasingly distant.

It's a wise writer who avoids going back to the beginning every day.

Francis Coppola, widely adored for his directing, also has credentials as a first-rate writer. He has a hard rule about rewriting. Write page one, and then place it face down, beside you. Write page two and put it, again face down, atop page one. In this way a writer should work his way through the entire script. In other words, according to Coppola, don't rewrite at all until you've got a complete first draft, no matter how awkward and unwieldy that draft may be.

Later, you'll rewrite.

To my own taste, and based on the habits of numerous working writers I have come to know, this rule is somewhat too harsh. When many writers sit down to address their day's task, the first thing they do is rewrite the work they did the previous day. Wisely, however, they resist the urge to go farther back than that.

With yesterday's pages rewritten, they can begin writing today's new pages. The next day they will rewrite today's pages and write an equal number of new pages. In this manner writers can leapfrog their way through a respectable first draft.

Granted, it's hard—for many writers perhaps even impossible—to resist looking only at yesterday's work before going on to today's. Yet too much preoccupation with previously written pages can prevent writers from moving forward in their tale; it undermines momentum.

Perhaps the most difficult part of rewriting is fulfilling the specifications of a producer. Most writers are, after all, only too aware that though they may have been paid money for their script, there's no guarantee it will actually be filmed. Sometimes, therefore, they all too eagerly agree to any and all changes suggested by their producer in the mistaken notion that this will somehow enhance the script's chance for production.

To be sure, some producers are tremendously adept at helping a writer find his way. But, sadly, too many executives ask writers for specific changes that even they themselves—the producers who are asking for the changes—do not believe in.

Why would anybody ask for such changes? Because too often executives are fearful that if they merely congratulate a writer on his performance, the producer will appear to be lacking insight and creativity. It requires a certain courage to read a draft and say: This is fine, let's shoot it.

Sometimes producers make up the suggestions as they go along. The script is basically fine but will be better if: all the characters are rewritten as Greek; the tale is reset in the future (or past, or present); the locale is changed from Ohio to Latvia, or the seventh moon of Saturn.

Writers, ever eager to please, ever eager to see their script move from ink on the page to light on the screen, too hastily agree. Greek? Of *course* the characters should be Greek. I'll have them all Greek for you by later this afternoon. The future? Sensational! Latvia? Perfect!

The problem here, of course, is that not only does such acquiescence not enhance the chances the film will be shot, it actually militates against them. This is because producers subconsciously want their writers to defend the creative choices manifested in their script. The producer paid the writer good money; he must be a good writer, he must have good reason for putting into the script whatever he has put into it. If a writer too willingly agrees completely and totally to amend those pages, where's his commitment to his work thus far? How soon will he abandon the writing he's embracing all so eagerly today?

The solution? I recommend writers adopt what I can only characterize as the yes—but approach. Yes, we can reset the tale in Latvia, but then we'll lose this, that, and the other thing. Yes, we can rewrite the characters as Greek, but then how do we explain this turn, that turn, and the other turn over there? Sure, we can set the story in the past, or future, but then we have to change all these fundamental aspects relating to qualities we once admired.

While writers ought never be intransigent regarding script changes and rewrites, neither should they abandon all backbone. Producers, aware of it or not, appreciate a writer who stands behind his writing.

That's why writers are wise to fall back upon what I call the old truth ploy. They serve themselves best by reacting to producers' questions and suggestions with honesty.

Experimentation

Writers can more easily deal with rewriting—indeed, with all aspects of creative expression—if they view a screenplay for what it truly is: an elaborate experiment.

Years ago I was writing a comedy for a studio. Having completed a first draft, I met with the director to discuss rewrites. After complimenting those aspects of the script he favored, he suggested areas that needed to be changed. As he went through the first of several such changes, I obediently checked off the sections that concerned him, eliminating passages he wished eliminated.

After a few moments he looked up and asked: "Aren't you going to argue with me?"

I told him that I would, just as soon as I disagreed with him. Maturing as a writer means more than merely learning to throw away; it means learning to *love* to throw away.

We continued reviewing the script and finally arrived at an area of disagreement where we nearly came to blows. Nevertheless, there blossomed a grudging mutual respect for one another. He didn't ask for changes just to ask for changes; I didn't pretend to agree with him when I did not, nor did I defend passages I regarded as indefensible. As in any collaborative enterprise, the individual artists' egos must become submerged in the collective ego belonging to the whole project.

How does a writer determine for once and for all whether or not a line, a character, a bit of action, or any other aspect of a script is worthy or worth chucking? Supposing there are—as indeed there often are—arguments on both sides, arguments for keeping a piece of material and arguments for discarding it?

The United States Department of Agriculture provides a wonderful rule. What does a citizen do upon opening a jar of home-preserved food only to discover something suspicious such as gas, discoloration, odor? Tasting even just the tiniest portion in the case of salmonella could cause a healthy adult to grow perilously ill. With botulism, it could just as easily prove fatal.

The USDA came up with a rule that serves not only home-perservers but also writers: *When in doubt, throw it out!*

Clearly, there's no problem including in a screenplay material that positively, absolutely is vital to the tale. Similarly, material that is certainly superfluous poses no problem. It's the in-between stuff that gets writers into trouble. But according to the USDA rule, a writer does not need to be certain that material is not needed; he need merely be uncertain. If there's doubt over whether to include a bit of business, lose that business!

Always err on the side of too much economy.

Sometimes writers anguishing over the appropriateness of a script's particular element might do well to take a blank sheet of paper, draw a line down the center, and put all the affirmative reasons on one side, all the negatives on the other. Often a pattern emerges, clearly demonstrating to the writer the need to keep—or lose—the bit.

Sometimes there is a danger here, too. There may be a host of reasons in favor of inclusion. And on the other side there may be but one lonely reason supporting exclusion. That single reason, however, may be important enough all by itself to warrant tossing the bit. For example, the one and only reason militating against a piece of business might be that it slows the story. But anything that slows a film story belongs in the wastebasket.

A writer cannot stand outside his script, intellectualizing about it, trying to figure out in advance what will work and what will not. He's got to roll up his sleeves and try things out. And if something ends up eliminated—a character, a scene, a line of dialogue—it does not mean the experiment was a failure.

Experiments are performed to determine a specific finding, to learn something, to discover some precise piece of information. Thomas Alva Edison tried all sorts of filaments for his light bulb, from sewing thread to human hair, until he stumbled upon tungsten and saw that it worked. Was the experiment with human hair a failure because human hair was a poor filament? Quite the contrary, the experiment was a complete success, because Edison found out what he needed to know, that human hair did not serve and he needed, therefore, to search further.

Screenwriting is not that different. If a writer tries something out and ends up throwing it away, the experiment can nonetheless be considered a success. The writer has determined what he needed to determine.

Word Processing

There has occurred in the past several years a genuine revolution in technology that is transforming the writing habit in ways previously unimagined. This is, of course, the advent of the personal computer.

Note, first, that I am the world's worst math-and-science cripple. I experienced no small trepidation, therefore, just a few short years ago when at long last I surrendered my typewriter and took up the cause of glowing green phosphor. I had become dreadfully aware that my screenwriting students at UCLA were leaving me behind. There was ample evidence in their screenplays—dot matrix printout, right margin justification, tractor-driven perforated paper—that they were becoming computer literate while I drifted daily further and further into history. The turning point came the day I heard my first electronic excuse for a missed deadline: "Sorry, Professor," the student told me, fully serious, "but the dog ate my floppy disc."

It was with fluttering heart and throbbing head that I finally bought what is by now already considered a steam-driven antique of a computer. Costing thousands of dollars at the time, a few short years later the identical model is given away free with an oil change.

Near tears, with trembling hands, I unpacked the boxes, wove the net of cables, powered up, inserted my first floppy.

I've never looked back.

Hardware—Which Computer to Buy?

It really doesn't matter which machine you purchase; the word processor market holds an embarrassment of riches. It is extremely difficult to make a serious mistake in purchasing a computer.

For writers who expect to use their computer exclusively for word processing, one needs as little as 64K on-board memory (never mind for now just what that means; know only that a typical bottom-of-the-line machine these days comes with four to ten times that). Required also is a pair of disc drives plus a low-level letter-quality printer.

Screen size is one factor that ranks high for writers. A screenwriter will spend tens of thousands of hours during his lifetime staring at that screen. At as little as twelve inches, the characters on screen are actually larger than scale, which is to say sufficiently easy on the eye.

For years I put off purchasing a computer simply because I thought I could not work on screenplays without at all times seeing an entire page of script before me (even though this is not possible even with a typewriter). Eventually I discovered that a whole page at a single scan provides too much information; it renders the writing unwieldy and confusing. The typical system, offering on screen perhaps forty percent of a page at a glance, is ideal.

Software

As is typical of computer purchases, my machine came "bundled" with a stack of discs and manuals so high that standing atop it could give a writer a nosebleed. I hasten to assert that to this day I have not so much as broken the cellophane sealing the programs and operating manuals except for the handful appropriate to screenwriting.

All a screenwriter really needs by way of software is his system's operating language and a word-processing program. Most likely he will also find quite useful a key-redefining program (more about all of these items in a minute). There is possible use also for a spell-check program integrated perhaps with an electronic thesaurus and possibly also a special screenplay formatter.

The System's Operating Language

Use of a system's operating language occupies less than one percent of a writer's time at the keyboard, but the subject has nevertheless to be addressed because without it a writer cannot get into that area where he spends the other ninety-nine percent: word processing. Happily, it is a lot less complicated than it sounds.

A system's operating language is that swarm of invisible codes and electronic cues by which the machine manages somehow to talk to itself. Writers, who tend to have more than ample experience talking to themselves, ought to be sympathetic with that part of the process. And once a writer has loaded his word-processing program, the operating system doesn't matter.

About the only use a writer will have for his operating system is to format his discs (prepare the blank discs to accept the screenplay—a process occupying mere seconds), and to prepare back-up copies for protection against loss.

Note, please, that it *is* important for writers religiously to make back-up copies of their writing. A computer can reproduce an entire script for electronic storage in a moment. And two back-up copies are better than one. Better still are two back-up copies stored in separate locations. What good are back-up copies all packed together in the same case when that case is damaged, stolen, or lost?

Note, also, that a computer copy is not a copy at all but actually a clone. Unlike carbons or photocopies, the four-hundredth generation—or the four-millionth—is exactly as clear and complete as the original disc.

It is important to make copies regularly because computers *do* offer new and frightful ways for writers to lose their writing—though writers have managed to lose entire screenplays long before there was green or amber phosphor, bauds, bits, and bytes.

The Word Processing Program

I still use the first word-processing language I ever learned, WordStar, which happens also generally to be considered the lingua franca of such programs. From time to time writers move on to other programs, but they all seem to start out with WordStar.

And I know many writers who, after having become

conversant with a broad selection of newer languages, eventually have retreated to WordStar. All writing, perhaps especially screenwriting, requires endless changes of heart, mind, and word. WordStar's beauty is that it permits writers to do just that—and with extraordinary ease.

With WordStar it is possible to insert language of any length and have the entire document instantly adjust itself so that everything fits just so. And WordStar makes it possible also to delete as little as a single letter or as much as an entire file. Still more important, the WordStar user can grab a fistful of language from any location within a script and move it anywhere else. This is called electronic cut-and-paste, since it's as if the writer were clipping out a section and pasting it elsewhere.

So WordStar is a great organizer.

The book you are reading was written in WordStar, and even before it was actually written its "topic modules" were electronically sorted, organized, arranged, rearranged.

Learning WordStar is relatively easy. New users need to know, however, that computer programs' operating manuals often appear to be precisely what they are: documents written by engineers for engineers. I recommend, therefore, that screenwriters without advanced degrees in engineering purchase what I call an idiot's guide to WordStar. There are more than several available, but it is hard to imagine that there can be any better than *Introduction to WordStar* by Arthur Naiman.

Naiman opens with a chapter called "A Taste of WordStar in an Hour." A writer knowing positively nothing about computers can, by following the simple instructions, actually write a real, true document, edit it, and print it out as hard copy, i.e., ink on paper. And instead of occupying the promised hour, in fact it requires all of some twenty minutes!

If a writer absolutely had to, he could go directly from that chapter to writing an entire screenplay, in a fraction of the time it would take on a typewriter. But I don't recommend it, as to do so would be to fail to exploit so many of WordStar's wondrous capabilities.

It surely pays to spend a morning or an afternoon—maybe even both—scanning Naiman and just playing around loosely with WordStar. But no attempt should be made to master the language simply from the book. As with any foreign language, WordStar is most effectively learned by following a decent guide at the same time as the student attempts to use the new tongue in a practical situation. Questions that arise in the course of such a method represent not intellectualization but application and are far easier for the mind and hand to grasp. Problems are solved exactly as they are confronted, and solutions are more easily, more permanently embedded in the user's brain.

Key Redefiner

A key-redefining program does just what the phrase suggests: It enables the writer to change the meaning of any and all of the keys on his keyboard. Indeed, it enables the writer to do this twice, because just as with a typewriter, each key has two positions: lower case and upper. For example, should there be a character in a screenplay named Susanna, the writer can redefine any of his keys—perhaps he'd want to use *S*—not only to type out the entire name at a single stroke but also to move the cursor (the electronic pencil point) to that next spot where the succeeding line of dialogue begins.

That may not strike a novice as a miracle on the order of loaves and fishes, but with a key-redefining program completely attuned to all the names in a particular script, whipping one's way through extensive dialogue exchanges by barely wiggling one's fingers is an unexpectedly slick, sexy experience.

But that is not what renders key redefiner truly useful to the screenwriter.

Screenplay format requires a forest of tab settings and specially customized margins—left, right, dialogue, parenthetical, character name, effects, and more. A writer normally has to set these every time he powers up his machine.

Worse, these settings and margins constantly change as the writer moves within a screenplay from description to dialogue and back again, endlessly throughout the script.

A key redefiner permits the writer to preset his various margins and tabs just once—a process typically requiring perhaps fifty key strokes each time—and then to switch effortlessly up and back among them as needed with a single flick of the finger. What's more, it enables his machine to "remember" the settings even with the power off, so that in the morning, when the writer boots up, the format is all set with just a couple of quick strokes.

My system uses Heritage Software's famous Smartkey. But there is a wide variety of such programs available, many among them quite capable and relatively inexpensive.

A Spell-Check Program

Many software bundles include some version of a program that electronically proofreads scripts for spelling errors. To my eye, every misspelled word is testimony to a script's carelessness. Having said that, readers may well be surprised to hear me advise vigorously against the use of computerized spell-check programs.

In the limited use to which I've put my own, I've found it far more valuable in locating typos than ill-spelled words. And, truth to tell, even its ability to do merely that is severely limited. If you erroneously write *fact* instead of *face,* no spell-checker will catch it, no matter how vast its vocabulary, for *fact* is perfectly acceptable—as well it should be—to any spell-check system.

Moreover, spell-checkers are not likely to recognize a host of movie script terms—EXT, INT, and so on. And while virtually every system permits you to add these and other terms to the system's glossary, it can be an annoying, grating process, first interrupting the writing as the "error" is "caught," and then requiring a decision as to whether it's worth taking up any of the amended dictionary's space with a particular term.

Even more problematic, it's nearly impossible to have every form of a word in a spell-checker. *Fall* is fine but how about *fallen, falling, falls?* Does a writer want to clutter up his program with all these combinations? Does he want his machine to pause and "ask" about each invocation of such a form? Does he want to squander his time and creative energy making endless extra decisions about which terms to keep and which ones to lose?

But the worst aspect of using electronic spell-checkers is that the process robs the writer of what ought to be among his most educational experiences, those endless and edifying journeys through that richest of writing resources: the dictionary. Words are all the tools a writer has. The dictionary is no less than an inventory of his arsenal. If writers don't perpetually expand their knowledge of language, if they don't love and protect and defend it, who will?

Still worse than a spell-check program is an electronic thesaurus or some other kind of integrated style program. These may actually beep a synthesized-sound reprimand at a writer who uses a particular term too often.

Myself, the first time my computer beeps at me I promise to slap its green, glowing face.

Special Screenplay Formatters

WordStar is as capable of printing a screenplay as it is of writing one. There is, however, one disadvantage. WordStar may split up a character's speech between the bottom of one page and the top of the next, which can render a script just slightly awkward in appearance.

There are today a host of screenwriting format programs adept at recognizing various features, such as dialogue, special to screenplays. And these programs allow a writer to avoid breaking the page mid-speech.

More than merely dealing with dialogue, however, a good screenplay formatter permits a writer virtually to scrawl out the entire movie at his keyboard in almost any fashion, as long as he follows a handful of simple rules. When the writer is ready, he replaces WordStar with the formatter in the first drive, presses a button, and watches as the script is transformed into neat, professional screenplay format within minutes.

One widely loved screenplay formatter, Scriptor, was developed by two screenwriting students from USC. Many screenwriters swear by it. Scriptor takes a mess of a draft and quickly rearranges it as a clean, responsible-looking script.

Avoid Fancy Printing Effects

Writers should avoid certain special effects word processing offers: boldface, right-margin justification, fancy and varied type fonts. Subliminally these tend to suggest the writer is not sufficiently confident about his story, characters, and dialogue, and hopes that decorating the script will somehow cover up more basic deficits.

The well-processed script should not look processed at all; it should look merely perfectly typed, and not a bit better than that.

PART IV
THE BUSINESS

9

SCRIPT SALES

STRATEGIES:

Dollars for Dreams

Teaching in a highly competitive program at an esteemed institution of higher learning brings me into close contact with many of screenwriting's sharpest, brightest students. They bring talent, discipline, language skills—the whole array of writing strengths—and they also bring a single glaring weakness: too much show business savvy.

Too Much Savvy

At the first meeting of an advanced screenwriting class at UCLA, each student briefly presents an overview of the screenplay he hopes to write for the course. I shall never forget one such session. One student had a father-and-son story; another had a tale about an artist making his way west after the Civil War. Another's concept involved restless youths thumb-tripping their way through outer space. If some notions were more promising than others, not one was on its face unworkable.

Then, offering not a shred of story detail, a student blithely announced that it was his intention to write a tale which, as he put it, "closely synchronizes with the profile of product sought by the new administration at" a particular studio. Sad to relate, the fellow was deadly serious. Like too many big-university, Hollywood-hip screenwriting students, he devoured the movie trade publications daily in an attempt to divine studio politics, personnel, and worst of all, current trends.

If ever there were a recipe for failure, it is that; it's the reason I confiscate the trades whenever I catch my students reading them. Trade publications have their proper place, to be sure, but each tends also in no small measure to constitute a catalogue of publicists' sweet lies, inventories of who's pretending to work on what purported project.

Writers hoping to impress agents or executives by cashing in on current trends are already too late. Today's trend was yesterday's innovation. This season's fad, whatever it is, had to be in the pipeline two years ago.

The lovely irony is that even in wicked old Hollywood, the wisest tack a writer can take is foolishly, recklessly to follow his heart and tell that story which is most personal, the tale unique to his experience and personality. No doubt, skittish writers seek refuge in trends because the tactic seems safe. But writing is risk. To reach audiences, writers have to take chances. They must confront the awesome challenge inherent in peddling fantasies. Every writer, in particular the new writer, faces the overwhelming likelihood that what he writes will come to no fruitful end. Instead of futilely attempting to diminish the risk, the smart writer embraces it.

The well-written script, even unsold, serves a multitude of purposes. The writer can use it as a sample of his craft in order to seek representation. He can offer it to production companies in the hope of winning funds—through a development deal—to write yet another script based on yet another idea. He can hope to land an assignment to rewrite somebody else's script. A good script should enable the writer to support his writing habit and confront the awful risk yet again.

Stated succinctly: *The smartest marketing strategy is good writing.*

Representation

At least once in his life every writer should visit a typical studio story department. Floor to ceiling, occupying every linear foot around the perimeter, stacked six to sixteen deep along the walls are scripts, thousands of scripts, scores of thousands of scripts. Fully ninety-nine percent of these screenplays remain unsold, and even among the precious few for which money has actually changed hands, the vast preponderance remain unproduced.

How does a writer get his script past that fortress of felled forests and into the hands of someone with the authority to film it? Must he seek an agent, or can he make direct submissions to production companies?

The answer is: Yes—he may seek an agent or he may make direct submissions to production companies.

Direct submissions to production companies, however, are often problematic. Generally, a script mailed unsolicited to a studio will be returned unopened and unread. Studios believe this protects them from nuisance plagiarism suits. Presumably, they cannot successfully be sued for stealing a script they have not read.

Most often, therefore, a writer's best bet to gain special attention and intelligent merchandising for his screenplay lies along the former path: He needs to have it represented by a reputable, responsible literary agent.

The roots of artists' representation lie in the ancient notion, partially justified and partially not, that creative souls—poets, painters, writers, composers—whose business is emotions are too sensitive to wallow to mundane matters like money. They must avoid at all cost, so the theory holds, bruising those delicate egos upon which their creativity depends.

But in truth writers should consider themselves working people, and working people need declare themselves masters of their own fate. Regardless of how high-hearted and sweet-minded a writer may be, it is a dreadful mistake for him to consider himself forever above the fray.

Notwithstanding any of this, in order that artists may both create their art on one hand and pay their rent on the other, over the ages there has arisen a cadre of representatives, business folk who, in exchange for their own piece of the action, act in the artists' behalf when confronting the merchants.

For one thing, working artists may well lack the time and spirit to wheel and deal in the professional arena and at the same time attend to their art. For another, presumably they do not possess the business acumen to appreciate the finer points of deal-making—rates, rights, complications. On its face, a professional arrangement to sell or develop a screenplay may seem simple enough: The producer agrees to pay the writer a certain amount of money in exchange for writing the screenplay.

But how much, if any, is to be paid in advance? How much on conclusion? Is there to be a bonus on commencement of principal photography? What precisely *is* "principal photography"? What is the fair size of such a bonus? Must the writer first prepare an outline for the producer's approval? What about rewrites and revisions? Can the producer fire the writer mid-project and hire someone else? And if that's the case (as it too often is), who gets what credit on screen?

How much money for the writer if and when the film is shown on television? What about the *second* time it is shown on television? And, for that matter, what about the three-hundred-and-forty-seventh such telecast? What about foreign rights? What about sequels? What about the producer's right of first refusal on the writer's subsequent project(s)?

Clearly, writers require expert advice in all these areas. They have every reason to expect that some substantial portion of such expertise may be provided by a responsible agent.

Recently I made the mistake of reading one of my own contracts. I say "mistake" because reading a contract can wrongly lead the writer to think he actually understands it.

To be sure, I own no such presumption. The contract could have been written in Navajo for all the sense it made to me.

A measure of the document's complexity can be found in a note on page one. Beyond mere salary, my agent had negotiated some number of "points," a percentage of the film's net profit. Beside the phrase *net profit* was an asterisk. At the bottom of the page was another asterisk and the legend: "For definition of Net Profit see Appendix A."

The contract itself was written on extra-long legal-sized paper positively aswarm with microscopic print, page after blinding page. And at the end of the contract, as promised, was the heralded Appendix A, "Definition of Net Profit." Need I relate that Appendix A was all by itself several times longer than the entire contract?

To attain a sense (sometimes false) that one's rights are fully protected, agents—and these days possibly also lawyers—are necessary.

Good Faith

But beyond agents, beyond lawyers, beyond personal managers, beyond convoluted contracts with complicated definitions of net profit, above all else what a writer needs is faith. The same faith necessary to write a screenplay in the first place is required also of writers who, having written that script, hope to navigate their way through the business. They have to be able to tolerate a certain uncertainty.

For without good faith, even the most carefully prepared, assiduously detailed contract is effectively meaningless. Even a major studio, for all its size, is often merely a cog among numerous enterprises owned by a far larger conglomerate. With its vast legal staff and boundless resources, it can effortlessly embroil a writer in endless, costly legal procedures year after year if it chooses to do so.

Not long ago a prominent writer enjoyed in his contract a

uniquely rich participation in his film's profit. The movie turned out to be a thundering success, earning more than one hundred million dollars. But the writer, though paid his original and generous fee, never saw a dime of what had to be a still far greater sum.

After costly audits of the studio's books by his own accountants, he sued.

In a television interview the head of the studio, defending his company's position, told a reporter that the artist had already received hundreds of thousands of dollars for scripting the movie. Where was it written, he wanted to know, that a writer should own part of the picture itself? I ached to hear the reporter respond: "Why, in the contract your studio negotiated with him." But the reporter remained silent.

The executive went on to challenge the writer. He had engaged the fanciest lawyers in all of Hollywood, he asserted, who had written him the lengthiest, most ironclad contract in show business history. Let him compel them now to enforce it. All parties would meet in court in the next century.

Into what useful information does this translate for new writers? Simply that they should forget about agents, lawyers, rights, contractual clauses, and profit provisions altogether, at least during the period they're actually composing their script. They have their hands full worrying about good writing.

Once they have written a worthy script, they can engage capable professionals to worry about these details for them. And as surely as they need constantly to confront the possibility a script will not sell, they need also recognize there is a possibility their rights will not be consistently upheld relative to a script that has won a contract. Writers—successful and not—had better be prepared now and again to have their hearts broken. If their sanity absolutely requires a consistently honest accounting plus unmitigated fair treatment they should stay out of the dreams-for-dollars business altogether.

Acquiring an Agent

The rule is that as long as you truly need an agent you'll never find one; conversely, if you don't need one, agents will queue up at your door pleading to represent you. Of course, this is a bit of an exaggeration, but only just a bit. Agents are not evil; they are merely human. And, if they are any good, they are also busy.

A writer friend of mine who has changed agents at least a dozen times in the past couple of years told me recently he's finally found one with whom he is truly happy. The agent calls him, my pal boasts, several times a week, just to chat and see how things are going. But frankly, I urge writers to beware of agents who have time to gossip; a writer wants his agent to be too busy beating the bushes for bucks to have time for time-passing conversation. It's perfectly fine, if rare, for agents and their clients to become truly close friends. But what counts first of all is not their personal but their professional relationship.

There are essentially two kinds of services an agent might realistically provide a client: find him a professional assignment, and sell a piece of original material the client has written. For most writers, especially new ones, as a practical matter agents offer only one of these services. And that is the second: selling original material.

But let's discuss the first service first. A writer without previous credits, much less a writer with no sample script to show anybody, has a snowball's chance in Southern California of finding a paid writing job. That's why it's largely a waste of time trying to work up a verbal story pitch or even to write a so-called treatment—a story synopsis told in the present tense—or any kind of proposal.

I should quickly tell, however, of a longtime friend, a former college professor of English who arrived in town with a proposal for a television series and questions for me as to what to do with it.

"Put it in a deep drawer," I recommended. "No studio

or network is going to buy a proposal from an unknown writer."

"But isn't TV interested in new ideas?" he asked.

"Do you watch TV?" I responded. "Does it appear to you that they're interested in new ideas?"

I said this not because I'm a snob about television. To my view, television is no different from theatrical feature films; most of it is pretty poor, and some small percentage is wonderful. This is the case, of course, for all creative expression.

I discouraged my friend even from sending his brief proposal to producers because I was certain it would be returned unopened and unread.

"But if they aren't interested in new ideas," he continued, "what are they interested in?"

"In people," I told him.

"What people?"

"The same people," I said, "who got a show on *last* year. They do not want to take chances with unknown writers who might produce a program that is mediocre; they want people they can *count on* to be mediocre."

"But the people who got a show on last year," my pal persisted, "each and every one of them at one time in their lives had never had a show on."

I told him that as an uncredited writer newly arrived in town, he should get to work speculatively writing a showcase feature-length screenplay, and accept the TV proposal as a warm-up, a worthy ten-finger exercise.

Disregarding my advice, he mailed his proposal blindly to a prominent television production company.

And two weeks later they bought the project.

I relate this incident because it is fair warning that any advice in this book may prove plain wrong when applied in a given instance. Bearing that in mind, I still stand on my advice: The way to get an agent is to speculate on a screenplay.

Speculating

If a writer sits down and writes a screenplay in exchange for which he receives not a dime or even the promise of a dime, the writer is said to be speculating. It's a fancy euphemism for writing for free. Oddly enough, speculating can be the craftiest marketing move a writer can make.

It is the way virtually every successful writing career is launched. This is because until a writer demonstrates that he can write—by writing something—no one is likely to hire him. Once he has written a screenplay, he alone owns one hundred percent of it. Among the entire film community only the writer can create a "property" out of nothing besides his own thoughts, whims, hunches. And if he is serious he must get started forthwith.

If the script turns out to be terrible and nobody wants to buy it, or if it turns out wonderful and *still* nobody wants to buy it, the writer can sit himself down and speculate another.

And he can speculate yet another after that.

While an agent almost certainly will not go out and peddle an unknown writer's services, if he feels the script is any good he may well hustle that same anonymous writer's existing screenplay. This is because even if the writer is unknown, the screenplay is not. For once it is written, it is there, in all its glorious (or not so glorious) pages. One can heft it in one's hand, thump it against a desk.

More important, one can read it.

And upon reading, one can love it, hate it, or a bit of both. But one need no longer guess about it. For there it is for all the world to see.

Hollywood Nightmares and Myths

In the film and television business one never has to stand in line awaiting his ration of heartache. As critic Pauline Kael puts it, Hollywood is the one place on earth where you can die of encouragement.

To be sure, Hollywood abounds with dark stories about how cruelly its artists are cheated, mistreated, and abused. And that, as they say, is the *good* news, for there is something far worse than that: neglect. Infinitely more painful than the harshest criticism is the yawning, hollow silence attendant on being ignored.

Tragically, too many Hollywood nightmares are true. But there are two popular perceptions that are in fact false.

Myth #1 is that screenplays—and even mere *ideas* for screenplays—are commonly stolen.

A modest movie is budgeted these days at fifteen million dollars. What's more, the fifteen million dollars necessary simply to get a modest movie shot is just the beginning. Those expenses are followed by an additional ten million or more merely for advertising and prints.

It ought to be evident that no movie studio is going to invest twenty to thirty million dollars on a movie for which the rights have not been secured. It makes no sense to run the risk of subpoenas, injunctions, and litigation of every kind, just to avoid spending even as much as, say, a quarter of a million dollars or more for the script.

From time to time perhaps something *does* get stolen, but this is most exceptional. Far more commonly, some writer *claims* that some particular film credited to others is in fact based upon something he wrote. A boy and a girl fall in love in the studio's movie; a girl and a boy fall in love in *his* script.

What possible explanation besides larceny?

Why do so many people seem to think their idea was stolen? Probably because they misunderstand the value of an idea. They do not realize that ideas, basically, are just ideas—brief, unformed flashes of incidents or insights, broad bits and pieces of notions.

Trembling with excitement, a friend of mine who happens to be a surgeon recently told me that he had "a great idea for a movie." All that remained, he assured me, was "for it to be written."

Because he is my close and affectionate friend, I resisted the urge to say to him: "I have a great idea for a kidney transplant; all that remains is the surgery."

As asserted in the chapter on work habits, ideas are cheap. What has value is an idea worked out in detail, not merely thought up but written down. It needs to be expressed on paper in such a way as to sustain and maintain interest and attention through a well-constructed plot integrating warm-blooded characters speaking crisp, trenchant dialogue in fresh, original scenes and settings.

New writers too often are afraid to show their work for fear it will be swiped. But new writers are best advised to "dazzle 'em with their footwork," show their work to anybody and everybody who'll look. Even if readers don't respond in quite the fashion hoped for, the writer's name is paraded before the industry's eyes; the writers begin to achieve status: They're current, they're in circulation, they're in the market.

A simple precaution writers can take is to register the script with the Writers Guild of America. Scripts can be registered in person or by mail; at this writing the fee for writers who are not Guild members is ten dollars. The Guild's Registration Office will accept a copy of the material, seal it, store it (possibly on microfilm). Should it ever be necessary (as it is in a minuscule number of cases, far less than one percent), the Guild will testify in court that on a particular date they had in their possession the material in question. It is up to the court, then, to study the material and determine whether theft has actually occurred.

Writers have enough to worry about without worrying about what they don't have to worry about. Character, dialogue, and story are questions worth worrying about. Plagiarism is not.

Myth #2 is that no one reads scripts.

With the virtual certainty that an unsolicited script submitted blindly to a studio will be returned unopened and unread, it is easy to conclude that not too many people in

Hollywood are eager or even willing to read a new writer's work.

But nothing could be further from the truth. First, as already suggested, it is probably a mistake for a writer to make his own submission directly to a potential purchaser. He's better off having an agent do that. And winning the attention and consideration of an agent is sufficiently difficult without making it more difficult than it actually is. While stamina is forever useful, reaching agents is a simple procedure.

The Writers Guild publishes and updates its franchised agency list every month. The list contains names, addresses, and phone numbers of approximately five hundred agencies. Some of these agencies are one-person operations. Many more involve several agents. Still others have dozens of agents representing writers. Collectively, then, the list provides access to literally thousands of writers' representatives.

All listed agents are licensed by the state and certified to abide by covenants negotiated with the Guild. To put it another way, the listing confers a certain legitimacy upon the agency. This is not to suggest that all agents will satisfy every writer; it means simply that no writer should deal with any agent who is *not* on the list.

How to get the list? Go to the Guild and ask for it; they'll hand it to you over the counter for free and with their best wishes. Can't come to Hollywood? Write to the Guild (Writers Guild of America, West, Inc.; 8955 Beverly Blvd.; Los Angeles, CA 90048) and enclose a stamped, self-addressed envelope; they'll mail it to you straightaway.

A glance at the list reveals that some agents indicate they do not accept unsolicited submission from writers unless they are recommended by persons known to them. Other agents indicate the reverse, that they welcome unsolicited scripts from first-time writers.

The majority, however, indicate nothing either way.

For the most part, writers may ignore these indications. If they will adhere to the simple method that follows, they should have relatively little trouble winning the consideration of agents.

First, permit me to make a suggestion that ought to seem obvious and yet is largely ignored by the bulk of new writers. *Do not try to reach agents by telephone.*

A former student of mine, now a prospering playwright and screenwriter, in her scuffling days got a part-time job working for a top agent. On one occasion, when his secretary was away from her desk, he asked the student to watch his phone during lunch.

Upon his return he asked if there had been any calls.

She handed him a list of one hundred and four calls; these were merely the calls that had come during lunch!

If Warren Beatty were on the list, you can be certain the agent would promptly return his call. If my name were among the callers, the agent would just as eagerly return my call. It is not because I'm as widely celebrated as Warren, or that I'm better looking. It is because from an agent's point of view, my call likely signals the recommendation of a promising new writer for representation.

But if a Doe calls (John or Jane) there simply is no earthly way the agent can return the call. It is impossible for a single human daily to return hundreds upon hundreds of calls.

To be certain, Hollywood is phone-crazy, obsessed with telecommunications etiquette. Who calls whom? Whose secretary calls whose secretary? Who comes on the line first? There is no escaping the importance of the telephone in the professional film and television writing world. For agents, it is an especially critical tool. More than any mere tool, it is a weapon. A leading agent compares it specifically to a bayonet.

Yet I caution writers against telephoning agents. How then do you win an agent's consideration for your screenplay without using the telephone?

You're a writer?

Write a letter.

The same top agent with a hundred and four calls during

lunch, the one who routinely ignores but an infinitesimal portion of them, nevertheless answers *all* his mail.

How can that be?

Prominent agents are by nature workaholics. Like them or don't like them—they work hard. If they feel particularly lazy one day, they'll delay their morning arrival at the office until six-thirty. The phones are miraculously quiet for thirty minutes (until the East Coast calls roll in). It's an opportunity to catch up with neglected matters. Most important for writers, it's an opportunity for agents to read their mail.

An agent grabs yesterday's stack, seizes his Dictaphone, and barks his responses. A phone conversation that would have eaten up fifteen minutes is disposed of in a terse nine seconds.

Even a letter from an unknown writer, a complete novice, gains its brief moment of scrutiny. If it's a lame letter the agent may pay the writer the respect of instructing his secretary to send the formal we-don't-read-unsolicited-scripts response. An intelligent letter, however, will almost surely win the response the writer seeks: an invitation to submit the script.

Clearly, the wording of such a letter—in publishing it's called a query letter—is crucial.

The writer ought to be aware that his letter is the first evidence of his ability—or inability—to write. It's the place to start exercising infinite care; it's the place to demonstrate an appreciation for the way one comes to be perceived by others.

Be certain the letter is economical, efficient, direct.

Most important: *Do not include the script with the letter.*

The letter should appear to have been written quickly, even breezily, but in fact the writer needs to spend perhaps several hours on getting it just exactly right. Happily, once such a letter is composed it can be copied and recopied, submitted and resubmitted to agent after agent.

But this does not mean it can be a form letter, addressed to-whom-it-may-concern. Though the writer eventually may send this very same letter to scores of agents, there should be no hint of that fact in the letter.

And of course it is imperative that the letter be typed.

To make the letter appear personal, the agent's name is required. You're writing to the agent, not the agency. Supposing you choose to approach, for no particular reason, Regressive Artists Agency; how do you know to whom to address it?

Here I renege slightly on my don't-use-the-phone injunction. Call the agency's switchboard and ask for the name of an agent at that particular agency.

And here follows a reconstruction of a letter written to agents by a film student some years ago.

> Dear Mr. Lastfogel:
>
> I am a student at UCLA in the Master of Fine Arts program in Screenwriting.
>
> I have written a screenplay, SHADOW CLAN, an action/adventure story set in contemporary New York City and ninth-century Scotland.
>
> I eagerly seek representation. May I send you the script for your consideration?
>
> Cordially,

Note that the first paragraph—one whole sentence long—introduces the writer in a brief but enticing way.

The next paragraph, also a single sentence, hardly describes the screenplay at all. It sets the genre, time, place, and nothing else. Who could refuse to read an action/adventure screenplay set in contemporary New York and ninth-century Scotland?

The letter then jumps right to the point, asking: Will you read this and consider representing it/me?

In the case of this particular writer, I had personally and enthusiastically recommended his script to a number of agents who promptly read it, and who just as promptly turned it down.

So much for *my* influence.

The agents seemed to appreciate the quality of the writing but were not sanguine about its chances to sell.

On his own, following my instructions, the writer sent his letter to several agents and *all* of them wanted to represent him. The writer went with the first one—not a terrifically respected agent at that—who nevertheless sold the script in a matter of days for three hundred thousand dollars to a major studio which—under a different title—proceeded to spend twenty million dollars producing the film.

Obviously, it's helpful in these letters to mention that the writer happens to be a student in a leading screenwriting program at a world center of higher learning. But what about a writer who has no such connection?

Here follows a variation on the theme.

Dear Mr. Lastfogel:

I am a probation officer for the city of Dayton, Ohio where, in my spare time over the past year, I have written a screenplay entitled BOTTOM DOLLAR.

It is an affectionate comedy about an AWOL marine's search for his long-lost father.

I eagerly seek representation. May I send it to you for your consideration?

Cordially,

Note that the final paragraph is identical to that in the previous sample. There is but a smidgen of information about the writer, just enough to make him appear interesting. Beyond the title is only the briefest description of the screenplay.

It is this last area where inexperienced writers get into trouble. They are all too eager to tell too much about their script. Instead, they should tease the agent, seduce him into wanting to know more. And the way to get him to want to know more is to tell him less.

The greater the detail you provide, the larger the target to shoot at. This is why you should never include a synopsis or outline of the script. If you provide a summary, it will only give the agent reason not to read the script. If you provide a summary, that's what the agent will read *instead* of the script. As eager as agents are to discover new talent, to say nothing of the prospect of earning generous commissions, they are also perpetually swamped with material and crave any excuse to avoid reading yet another screenplay.

Still, a well-crafted query letter will win nine out of ten agents' invitations to submit a script. It is in this manner that an unsolicited script becomes solicited.

Once the agent answers, agreeing to consider the material, the writer can send the screenplay with a quick cover letter. This second letter simply acknowledges the agent's own letter and indicates that, as requested, the script is enclosed.

Agents and the Law

Once a writer succeeds in winning representation, is there any danger the agent will not truly and faithfully work for the client?

It happens all the time.

Yet it is nothing to lose sleep over.

The worst thing that should happen to a writer ought to be that he wants to separate from his agent but his agent doesn't want to let him go. This occurs only when the client is earning sizable fees and the agent is motivated, therefore, to keep him.

It happens rarely.

Even in such an unusual instance, stuck with an agent he's come to dislike, the writer enjoys substantial protection. For one thing, literary agents in movies and television are by law limited to commissions of ten percent. I've never heard of an agent charging less, but under the law none charges more.

And commission means just that, a percentage paid out of the gross once a sale of original material or an agreement regarding writing services is consummated and the funds actually paid. To that end, no writer should ever send an agent any money. Neither should any agent charge a writer a nickel merely to consider representing a screenplay. No reputable agent will ask you for funds in advance.

And beyond the ten percent commission limit, the law also restricts agent/client contracts to ninety days unless there is a bona fide offer of employment. This means that even a writer not yct halfway through a two-year agency contract is free to leave if three months pass without an offer of a professional writing job.

The most common agent abuse by far is no abuse at all but, rather, neglect.

Agency Contracts

Many writers' contracts with their representatives are verbal. Oddly, new writers often appear disappointed if they do not have a written contract with an agent, if they are not "signed" by the agent.

But there is no reason in the world for a writer to have a signed contract with his representative. If there is nothing wrong with having such a contract—and there is not—neither is there any reason for the client to press the agent for papers, for it is primarily the agent who is protected by the agency contract.

This is a far cry, of course, from an agreement for employment. With employment, as opposed to representation, a contract is essential.

Cynical writers suggest that agents are like underwear; you should change them once a year whether you need to or not. Of course this disserves the legions of fine agents who capably and honorably service the professional screen-writing community. Still, it is worth noting that while there is something to be said for having a single representative throughout a career, in fact clients and agents frequently separate, often without hard feelings.

At the time of this writing, I have had more than a dozen agents, some of whom I've genuinely forgotten (to be fair, surely they have forgotten me, too). Among all these agents, I had signed papers over the years with perhaps a third of them. I'm not unwilling to sign an agency contract, but given my druthers, unsigned status is preferred. When agents have insisted I sign, without hesitation I have signed. But, again, the contracts simply do not mean a lot since the salient features—commission, term—are fixed by law.

Releases

From time to time writers, especially (but not exclusively) unrepresented writers, in order to have a screenplay considered may be required to sign a document called a release.

Should they sign it?

Yes.

A release is a legal document of no real consequence. Lawyers insist it protects production companies against nuisance plagiarism suits, but in my view this argument is largely unfounded.

A release purports to promise the producer that the writer is fully aware there may be scripts similar in concept and design to the one he is himself submitting. Should a disagreement arise as to authorship of another of the producer's projects, the writer pledges not to litigate but to seek instead some sort of arbitration.

Studio releases run to various lengths, from less than a single page to six or eight extra-long pages of impenetrable party-of-the-first-part legalese in gritty micro-print. The most benign represent a simple acknowledgment by the writer that there are probably similar projects; the most malignant state that should there arise a disagreement between the company and the writer, it is up to the sole discretion of the company to determine whether or not the writer's material was purloined.

But leading entertainment business attorneys assure me that no judge in any court will ever agree that a writer intended to assign his screenplay's rights to a studio in exchange merely for its agreeing to consider the project. In practical terms, therefore, a signed release means nothing. Regardless of its wording, the writer does not surrender his right to litigate, nor does he award to the studio the right to steal his writing.

Until recently, the general rule has been that no release was required from a writer whose work was submitted to a studio through an agent. Lately, however, even that seems to be changing; companies increasingly insist on releases even when the work is submitted through an agent.

But as noted earlier, writers have enough to worry about without worrying about what they don't have to worry about.

And releases are worth no worry. Since many companies flatly refuse to read material for which releases are not signed, there is every reason in the world quickly to affix a signature.

Purchase, Option, and Turnaround

A writer working on a paid assignment—developing a screenplay based upon a producer's idea, rewriting somebody else's script, adapting for the screen material from another medium such as a novel—is considered a "writer for hire" who does not truly have rights to the material upon which he works. If he did not originate the material he is merely a hired hand participating in a quid pro quo enterprise; the producer supplies the money, the writer provides the talent and toil.

Being a writer for hire, especially a well-paid writer for hire, is a wholly honorable proposition. But creating original material—in the case of new writers this almost invariably involves speculation—automatically results in the material's rights accruing to the writer. As long as he doesn't base the work on anybody else's copyrighted material, a writer owns what he writes.

Generally, once he's written something original, a professional writer devoutly hopes to sell it to somebody else. Best of all is to find someone willing to part with a fortune. Such an arrangement is characterized simply as "purchase." It is not much different from the purchase of anything else: a car, a coat, a pack of chewing gum. They have money, you have the product; they give you the money, you give them the product.

The purchase of original material for the screen is inevitably more complicated than that, to be sure. There are often bonuses based upon the material actually going into production. Perks and bumps—which is to say more money—are awarded if the material earns a certain amount of profit, or is parlayed into one or more sequels, or spins off into ancillary products—toys, shirts, posters, coffee mugs. And these extra benefits are not mutually exclusive; any combination of these happy occurrences may serve to enrich a writer who is skillful, insightful, to say nothing of lucky. The ancillary rights to *Star Wars*, as an example, were worth far more than the film's mere ticket sales, record-shattering though the latter happened to be.

Should a screenplay be purchased and never make it to the screen (a major studio typically buys at least fifteen screenplays for every movie it actually produces), there is some arrangement for reversion, or turnaround, of the film's rights to the writer. Some years ago the Writers Guild negotiated automatic reversion for writers, based upon a complicated formula involving time and money. Essentially, after seven years of nonproduction, the writer has a two-month "window" during which time he can return the money and reclaim the rights. Then, of course, he is entitled to sell those same rights to somebody else if he can find a willing buyer.

These rules regarding reversion represent the recognition by writers and producers alike that a screenplay is in fact *not* a car, a coat, or a pack of chewing gum; that if a producer fails to produce the film, the writer has the right to try to get the project produced elsewhere.

One might expect that the original purchaser should not object to such an arrangement; indeed, he ought to welcome it. His money is returned. In fact, however, many producers despair to see somebody else produce a project they once owned. In a business where appearance is all, it looks bad for a producer to be unable to get a project filmed and then have some other producer succeed with the same material. Worse still, God forbid that in such circumstances the movie should become a major hit!

Purchase of original material is rare, however, when compared to an option, which costs a producer a lot less than a purchase. It enables him to treat the material in very much the same manner as if he had purchased it outright. A producer wins the right to purchase the original material later, within a prespecified period and at a predetermined price. A producer not willing to risk a hundred and fifty thousand dollars on a particular screenplay might find the writer willing to let him option the material for substantially less.

It might very well be to the writer's advantage to accept such an arrangement. For one thing, the writer likely has tried, on his own or through his agent, to find a buyer. As happens with the overwhelming majority of screenplays, this proves futile. If after several potential purchasers have turned down the opportunity to buy the script outright, the agent and/or the writer may be reluctant to have the property exposed all over town, only to demonstrate conclusively that nobody wants to buy it.

There might, however, be a producer who feels that perhaps properly "packaged"—more about this later—with the right director and a star or two, or in some way rewritten, or for any host of reasons, the property is worth acquiring at least temporarily, in order to determine whether a movie might eventually result.

By obtaining an option, the producer rents rather than purchases the rights to the material. Instead of coming up with tens of thousands, or hundreds of thousands of dollars, the producer may instead offer much less, during which time the writer assigns him the project's rights plus the right, after six months or a year or two, whatever is negotiated, to purchase the project outright for a more substantial sum.

Typically the option payments are credited against the purchase; this is to say they are deducted from the final payment. And the time period is adjustable. It may be six months or a year, at a particular price. It may be renewable at the producer's discretion, perhaps at an adjusted sum for another period.

More important than the money paid for an option is the fact that once a producer acquires material he may actually devote time and attention to showing the script around to organizations with the capability to get the project filmed, such as networks and studios. He may also expose the script to directors and actors. In so doing, he may succeed in getting the script to the screen. Even if he fails at that, the writer's name and writing skills are demonstrated in various offices where they might otherwise not have been viewed. And the writer can report truthfully that a particular company has acquired the rights, however temporarily, to his script, conferring professional status upon a previous amateur.

It is more prestigious to have a legitimate producer, who's gone to trouble and expense, however small, of acquiring a script, peddling the property through the professional community compared to having the author himself or the author's representative doing the same thing. It demonstrates that somebody besides the writer and his

agent—both of whom have an obvious vested interest—
believe the screenplay is worthy of an audience.

As an example, a student at UCLA optioned a comedy
to a prominent producer. The producer, thanks to an extraordinary record of hit films, was able to have the script
read promptly at the highest levels of the industry. And
while no studio saw fit to produce this particular story, they
were favorably impressed with the writing.

The producer never succeeded in getting the film made
and eventually allowed the option to expire, which is the
fate of the overwhelming majority of options. But as a
result of the script being read at one specific company, the
writer won his first professional assignment: a rewrite of
another project. And since the writer had never worked
professionally before, and since he had no record of successful films, he was paid merely five thousand dollars a
week with a six-week guarantee, all this just to rewrite
somebody else's work.

Not too shabby for a first job.

And in fact, he ended up spending not six but eight
weeks on the rewrite, pocketed forty grand, kept the original option money for himself *and* the rights to his original
script. This writer, in addition to the cash, plus the en-
hancement of his reputation, enjoys the never-ending possibility that he may eventually sell the script all over again.

Even if he doesn't eventually find a purchaser who'll
acquire the script outright, there's always the possibility
he'll find someone else who wants to option it yet again. A
friend of mine had a script he wrote on assignment for a
producer at a major studio more than fifteen years ago.
Long before he finished writing, the producer was fired
from the studio. The company, honoring the writer's contract, paid him all the money owed, then promptly put the
project into turnaround; the rights reverted to my pal.

Of course, he wished the script had been filmed, but he
had no serious cause to complain. He was paid the full fee
as required in his contract, and still owned the rights to
what he had written.

Over the subsequent decade he sold six options on that same script and was nearly disappointed when, finally, it was once again purchased outright by another studio. I say disappointed, because over the years he'd grown used to renting out the rights. He had come to regard it as a kind of annuity and in time it had begun to add up to a respectable sum.

Finally, the new studio changed administrations, and the script went into turnaround yet again, the rights once more reverting to the writer. Here's a script, then, that effectively has been sold outright twice, has been optioned half a dozen times, and to which the writer still retains all rights plus the possibility it will sell—or be optioned—yet again, and maybe even again.

Writers sometimes sell options on material to producers virtually for free. Instead of stone, cold free, it's actually for one dollar. This is because legal agreements require that some sort of tangible exchange, however small, occurs between the parties.

Why in the world would a writer sell an option for his material for free (or for a dollar)? Because the producer may succeed in setting up the project to be filmed, in which case substantial remuneration accrues to the writer. Clearly one might be reluctant to permit the first person who reads material to option it; a writer with virginal material, a script shown to nobody, wants to get at least a sampling of opinions and reactions before agreeing merely to rent the rights for a relatively small sum instead of selling them outright for far more money.

If all else fails, if nothing comes of the optioned material, the writer has not hurt himself; he still retains all rights to the script and can hope to market it throughout his lifetime. There are scripts that have been around many times and for many years before they finally became films.

Packaging

You may have thought a movie is a movie, but it's not; in contemporary Hollywood parlance a movie is actually a package. You may have thought actors are actors and directors are directors, but they are not. An actor—especially a star—is an element. Likewise, in the scheme of movie things a director is not a director; he is but one more element. Similarly, you may have thought a screenplay is a screenplay, but it is not. A screenplay is a vehicle.

In the old days, into the late forties, when studios owned their own theaters, they also owned their own writers, actors, and directors. These artists did not operate freelance, picture by picture, studio by studio as today. Instead, they were on a single studio's staff and ordered by the studio to work on specific pictures.

Under such circumstances some artists came to consider themselves slaves, but no slaves were ever treated and paid so well. What's more, they enjoyed each other's companionship and support, a far cry from today's film industry wherein screenwriters live and work in veritable isolation.

There is today at every studio a so-called Writers' Building, a structure that once housed writers' offices but is now used for other purposes, usually to house independent production companies. And there used to be at every studio commissary a writers' table where, by tradition, the writers all ate lunch together every day of the week. Writers engaged in daily story conferences, bounced ideas and dialogue off each other, consulted collectively on any and all aspects of their work, from specific quirks of character to basic questions regarding story structure.

In those times a studio decided to make a picture, assigned the various artists, and made the picture. Today, more often than not, a picture finally comes into being bankable because elements become attached to a vehicle and form a fundable package.

Some years ago, Elizabeth Taylor was a bankable element. Elizabeth Taylor plus, instead of a script, the list of ingredients on a box of Raisin Bran, was a "go" package in Hollywood. A common misconception about bankability holds that audiences can be counted on to support a bankable element's pictures. This is simply not true.

There is in fact not a producer or director who means anything to audiences, at least to the extent that audiences can be counted upon to purchase tickets to his films. Not even George Lucas's name above the title could rescue *Howard the Duck*.

Interestingly, throughout film history the only director who ever could be depended upon to boost box office receipts was Alfred Hitchcock, and that was due only to his status as a television personality with his own weekly anthology show. It was only then, in his latter career, with the TV show a regular video staple, that studios widely publicized his name when releasing his latest film.

If any element means anything to audiences it has to be an actor, a star. Yet there isn't even a bankable star—not Clint Eastwood, not Paul Newman, not Barbra Streisand, not Meryl Streep—who hasn't been in pictures that failed. Not too many years ago *The Electric Horseman,* directed by Sidney Pollack (*Tootsie, Out of Africa,* and other substantial hits) and starring Robert Redford and Jane Fonda, sank like a stone. Somewhat more recently, Eddie Murphy with Dudley Moore in a screenplay (*Best Defense*) from one of Hollywood's richest writing teams (*American Graffiti, Indiana Jones and the Temple of Doom* among others), vanished without a trace.

So it is useful to remember that what makes an element bankable is not that audiences will flock to it but that bankers will bank on it. And if bankability is good news for this season's handful of hot elements, for movies in general it's no cause to rejoice.

Today, the pity is that packages of bankable elements prevail over movies. This is due to the necessity for studio executives to cover their tails in the event—no mere possibility but the vast likelihood—their picture fails. If a producer's project bombs, he does not have to justify squandering forty million of the corporation's dollars if he can point to Redford, Fonda, Pollack.

Bankable elements exist, therefore, for the purpose of assigning blame.

Lamentably, movies in many cases are now from inception not much more than elaborate schemes to prepare for their expected failure. Instead of exciting new ideas, studios search for packages of bankable elements to explain away films' predicted failures. Is it any wonder so much movie fare appears stale and listless?

What does this all mean for writers?

First, that a script—regardless of its strengths—submitted all by itself to potential purchasers is simply not likely to sell, much less likely ever to become a movie on the screen. Elements are necessary.

Writers still need to write the freshest, most original, most unique material they can write, but they must at the same time be prepared eventually to deal with agents and packagers and, especially, options, because what typically occurs during the option period is that the bankable elements are assembled.

This provides writers with extra reason to create characters who are broad, rich, fleshy, the sorts of roles bankable actors would like to play. But then good characters are already a basic tenet of good writing.

Should a writer be represented by an agent who also packages? It's a strategic toss-up. The big, powerful packaging agencies understandably prefer to represent not merely a script alone but also the director and the stars.

Why settle for one commission when you can own several?

Being a client of such an agency has its strengths and weaknesses. The elements for a full-blown package, perhaps even an on-the-screen movie, are available. But should one or another element fall out—as they almost inevitably do—suddenly the blush is off the project. The agency sees now perhaps only the script, and what packaging mega-agency wants the relatively meager commission on a script alone?

This is why writers, especially new writers, may be best off with smaller, more boutique-like agencies where a motivated representative might stage the sort of terrorist raid upon a studio required to get a picture started. Additionally, at the bigger agencies the individual writing client is all too easily lost in the shuffle of actors, directors, writers, writers, and writers.

Perhaps the best compromise is a new agent at a respected old(er) agency. When he calls potential purchasers they appreciate he's legitimate, yet he's still sufficiently motivated to establish his own reputation by establishing that of his clients.

At UCLA I frequently take calls from new agents just starting out at well-established agencies. They eagerly seek clients. I send them our best and brightest writers and for a brief period, for the most part they do great things. But soon, their stables fill, their reputations solidify, and they have only limited time to work for new artists.

The Writers Guild

The mainstream motion picture industry is a union shop. Film and television writers are represented by The Writers Guild of America, which maintains branches both in New York and Los Angeles. But although the networks and studios agree to employ union members exclusively, no potential employer will reject a writer simply because he's not a member of the Guild. This may appear to be a contradiction, but it is not. The writer simply agrees to join the Guild, once he negotiates his first sale or assignment.

New writers, therefore, have a leg up compared to new actors, directors, editors, cinematographers, carpenters, electricians, and makeup and wardrobe artists. This is because the Writers Guild will admit any writer to membership as soon as he wins an assignment from a signatory company.

Every legitimate company engaging a writer promptly notifies the Guild. The Guild checks its roster. If the writer is not a member, he is promptly invited to join. But the Guild will never propose to potential employers that they use instead writers who are already union members.

This is not at all the case for, say, editors. Should a company, impressed with the work of a particular new cutter, hope to have him edit their latest movie, they cannot blithely hire him. The editors' union, upon checking its roster and discovering the proposed candidate is not a member, will suggest that the producer use instead one of its available (unemployed) members.

In practical terms, this is good news for writers. New writers, having won their first assignment, may not want to be bothered worrying about matters like union representation. But the Guild is essential to guaranteeing responsible wages and working conditions, and writers' rights to such representation were won only after decades of truly heroic struggle.

Until there was a writers' union, screen credit depended upon the whim of the producer. Producers could (and did) arbitrarily assign writing credit to their spouses, siblings, children, and dogs. Now, as for the past several decades, credit is determined exclusively by the Guild. And on-screen writing credit is no small consideration. For writers, far beyond the emotional and psychological implications, screen credit is a measure also of money.

The Writers Guild of America represents, therefore, a no-lose situation for screenwriters, even for first-time screenwriters who do not yet belong. These writers are afforded all the Guild's protections and yet are not discriminated against even though at the time of first sale or assignment they do not belong.

As with all other technical and business considerations, writers can forget about how to get into the union and concentrate instead upon writing their best screenplay. That's because writing their best screenplay *is* the way into the union.

The Gatekeeper Theory

Since the film and television industry is so competitive, and prestigious, and glamorous, many of its on-the-line laborers are overworked and underpaid; they're willing to tolerate all sorts of abuse for the opportunity to work in so challenging and (sometimes) creative an arena. This is particularly true of office personnel, particularly receptionists, secretaries, clerks, and even janitors.

But these same people often wield substantial power!

In an effort to reach higher-ups—either by mail or telephone—it can be a serious mistake to run roughshod over them, for two reasons. First, running roughshod over people is simply not acceptable behavior among civilized adults in enlightened societies. Second, these lower-echelon functionaries often hold the key to influence and attention far beyond their own narrow sphere.

When I was still a student at USC's Cinema Department in the late sixties, I worked briefly as a script consultant to the head of a major studio. Soon, my boss ran the studio into the ground and was fired. Of course he was then promptly hired by another major studio, where he lasted several years until he ran *that* one into the ground, too.

During his tenure at the second studio, I attempted to reach him in order to have him consider a screenplay I'd written. I reached, instead, his secretary. In an aggressive, inconsiderate manner I figuratively tried to shove my way past her on the phone. The secretary hesitated and then, recognizing my voice, spoke my name. It turned out to be the same secretary he'd had at the previous studio, a woman I'd come to know well, and one capable of getting my script to the top of the pile of material on his desk.

Forgiving my rudeness, the secretary treated me generously, and arranged to have the script considered immediately. The boss read it promptly and just as promptly rejected it.

But the lesson still obtains. My firsthand familiarity with

this particular secretary—and her uncommon tolerance—spared me the wreckage of my bad manners. It pays, therefore, to be a decent, respectful human being, even in the movie industry. Agents' and producers' secretaries and their readers are generally abused by traffic at both ends of the line. That may explain why they are open to kindnesses even merely of tone and effect. These same badly treated folks often hold the key to the attention of very important people.

Make every one of them your ally.

When you call, ask for the precise name of the person with whom you're speaking, and jot it down for future reference. Kibitz with him or her for a moment; these folks are used to being pushed around and most will go the extra mile for a struggling writer who regards them with respect. Remember that in correspondence it is he or she who'll open the mail, deciding which matters merit the attention of the boss. And it's not a bad idea, therefore, to remember them fondly to their boss when you correspond.

In Hollywood, as elsewhere, your selfish best interest is served when you treat people selflessly

Professionalism

The difference between an amateur and a professional is that the former does it for free while the latter gets paid.

There is, of course, a significant difference between amateur and amateurish writing. A disciplined, talented amateur may write far more effectively than a particular pro, and a particular pro may write amateurishly. A professional's writing is not necessarily better than that of an amateur, it is merely more remunerative. And if no screenwriter needs to apologize for reaching an audience, neither need he apologize for getting paid to write.

At UCLA's Division of Film and Television my telephone rings constantly with would-be producers seeking writers who are "bright, fresh, new, innovative, not locked into any rut, not yet caught up in the whole Hollywood maw." What the caller often means is that he seeks writers who'll work for free.

When I casually ask how much money they're willing to spend, there is an astonished silence and the telephone grows palpably hot in my hand. Invariably the voices on the phone manage to mumble that they offer a new writer far more than mere money. They claim to offer access to studios and agents; they offer an almost ready-made deal that merely requires the "fleshing out" (a euphemism for writing) of a script.

"The whole story's set," many tell me, and some may actually believe it. "The characters are there. All that remains is to connect the dots. It needs merely to be put into screenplay format." At this point I suggest they hire a stenographer—it shouldn't cost more than six or seven dollars an hour—and, since it's all "worked out," the caller can simply dictate the script. The stenographer can get the whole thing done in a day for well south of a hundred bucks. As far as screenplay format is concerned, if the stenographer can't handle it, there are inexpensive software programs that will properly format the script in minutes.

The self-styled producers hem, haw, and then reluctantly admit that perhaps a *little* more than mere stenography is required—dialogue, for example, settings, conflict, characters, incidents—and besides, truth to tell, they can't in any case hire a stenographer because they lack even the hundred.

But what movie, I ask them, costing even just a couple of million dollars—a *super* low budget these days—ever gets made that requires a script be written for free?

"Students have to be prepared to speculate if they're going to get into this business," I'm informed gently and not so gently by my callers.

But my students speculate all the time, I explain. The difference is they own one hundred percent of what they speculate.

New writers need to keep in mind a simple but critical

principle: *If you want others to treat you as a professional, you must treat yourself as a professional.*

New writers should never become involved speculatively, therefore, in projects they do not entirely own. They must not allow themselves to get talked into adapting for the screen a play, for example, or a novel, if they do not possess the rights to the original material. And neither should they rewrite anybody else's screenplay in behalf of an erstwhile, would-be producer, in the hope that eventually they'll receive some decent cash, as well as a hefty on-screen credit.

For if the producer reneges (the overwhelming likelihood with material procured for free), the writer can't even market the fruit of his labor because he does not own it.

Self-appointed producers love to promise naive new writers all kinds of screen credit. But every legitimate producer knows, and every writer absolutely *must* know, that screen credit is determined exclusively by the Writers Guild through an elaborate system of confidential arbitration panels. The reason the Guild has labored so many years to capture this power is precisely to prevent producers and would-be producers from dispensing screen credit to writers like tips to the valets who park their cars at their power breakfasts.

The sometimes sweet, sometimes painful irony regarding money and writing is that the more a producer is required to pay a writer, the better he appreciates that writer's work. It is a self-fulfilling prophecy: I'm paying the guy real folding money; he must be pretty good. Would a crafty, tasteful, artistic producer like myself pay actual dollars to some hack?

And the converse is every bit as true. A producer who has a writer working for him for free will likely figure he's getting his money's worth. If the writer doesn't think his stuff's worth anything, why should the producer?

New writers commonly expect that if they demand to be paid they will be ridiculed. But to the contrary: The more confident a writer's insistence he be paid, the greater the respect the producer will afford both him and his work.

Obviously, no serious professional should get into any kind of discussion about money with a producer; he should put the producer in touch with his agent. For if a legitimate producer sincerely wishes to hire a writer, he should be not reluctant but eager to contact the writer's representative.

And no writer with a serious offer of employment ought to have any trouble engaging an agent. Indeed, he ought to be able to select precisely his agent of choice. This is because agents are understandably reluctant to expend the time-consuming effort shopping material from producer to studio to network. But no agent will reject a writer who walks in off the street with a deal in his hand.

Nobody turns away business at the door.

The writer is allowed to hope, even to expect, that the agent will negotiate a deal at least ten points better than the writer would have won on his own, thereby covering the commission.

A Secret among Writers

Respectfully, I must plead with producers who might stumble upon this volume to skip this section.

Writers will never say so—and well they should not—but no writer ever got paid, even as little as Writers Guild scale, who didn't have to restrain himself from howling at his producer: "Money? For this? You're nuts! These are just words. This is just writing. These are just ideas, thoughts, concepts, notions I wrote down. The characters in this script? I made 'em up! The story? Lies! How can you trade me money for my dreams? How can you trade me so *much* money?"

A Final Solution to the Agent Problem

Agents are people too.

There is something fundamentally difficult in the very nature of the agent/client relationship; it is in many ways a classic double bind. I expect it derives in no small part from the fact that there should be no real trick to selling material that's good, fresh, and innovative.

So it is all too perfectly human for the agent to downplay the quality of writing he attempts to market. At the same time as he wants the work to be good, he doesn't want it to be *too* good, because if it is, what's *his* job? Is he but a broker trading commodities? The better the writing, the paler the testimony to the agent's own prowess as a wheeler-dealer. Psychologically, therefore, he has a curiously vested interest in trivializing the quality of any client's effort.

As if that were not sufficiently awkward, there is yet another bind, equally irreconcilable.

Writers and agents alike will tell you that the client employs the representative, not the other way around.

But with whom, in fact, does the agent play tennis and sit in the sauna? The client? Rarely. More often than not, the agent socializes with management—producers, executives, studios, networks. And that's exactly as it ought to be, and it is exactly as every client ought to *want* it to be, because, as Willie Sutton replied when asked why he robbed banks, that's where the money is.

I submit that one obvious area of conflict between agents and clients could be quickly eliminated if the agent represented instead of the client merely the project.

Typically, to represent even a single project, the agent takes on full representation of all the client's writing. Among these projects are those for which the agent has great enthusiasm, and those for which he does not. It is fair to neither agent nor client to have a project represented reluctantly. Agent and client alike ought to have the right to forgo representation regarding this item or that one, perhaps with the agent possessing a version of first-refusal rights.

In too many ways an agent's lot is not a happy one; it's enough to evoke sympathy even among writers. For like the waiter who gets scolded by the kitchen (even though *he* didn't order the food) and scolded by the diners (even though *he* didn't cook it), agents take the heat from movie and TV producers for writers' shortcomings, and they take the heat from writers who blame them not for their own but for the producer's (from time to time somewhat) unreasonable demands.

Even agents need love.

CONCLUSION

THE WHOLE PICTURE

10

EMOTION:

Ego, Criticism, Rejection

and Heartache

Film is for feeling.

There's more to it than that, of course, but first and last there is that. And what audiences feel need not be pleasure. Frighten the folks, make them cry, make them angry; they will stand in line to see your movie. Human beings need regularly to experience strong emotions; it's how we come to remember we are alive. And as surely as muscles atrophy from disuse, so also do feelings.

Consider the movie theater, therefore, a gymnasium for the senses. It is an arena not for serenity and logic, not for intellect and reason, but for passion.

In his hugely insightful *Ascent of Man,* mathematician and philosopher Jacob Bronowski posits an insightful theory into film's nature. The caves at Altamira, Spain, whose walls are emblazoned with primitive paintings, were not domiciles, Bronowski notes. The tribes retreated to the caves from time to time for the exclusive purpose of viewing the paintings.

The paintings' subject is the local fauna, in particular the bisonlike creatures that were the hunters' prey. The hunters' very survival depended upon success in the hunt. The animals' flesh provided protein; the skins supplied shelter and clothing. But the beasts bore lethal racks of antlers with which to gore predators. They strode on hooves easily capable of trampling men. How could mere humans, Bronowski inquires, conquer animals stronger, larger, swifter than they?

The hunters' advantage was that special trait belonging to humans alone: the intellectual ability to cooperate and devise strategy. Stealthily they would surround the herd. Then, at precisely the proper moment, they would drive its members in the direction of comrades lying in wait, armed with spears.

But what would a man, even one holding a spear, be likely to do when faced by a herd of charging buffalo? The natural reaction would be panic and flight.

The hunters needed, therefore, to learn how to control and overcome that panic. They needed to train their emotions so that instead of fleeing they would stand their ground. The caves provided a place for the hunters to rehearse their feelings. The chambers were a safe arena to experience intensely frightening emotions without authentic risk.

The inner enclaves housing the paintings were accessible through twisting, turning tunnels that rendered them completely dark; light was provided by tallow-fueled torches. With the torches flickering very much in the manner of a movie projector, the images must have appeared to be in motion. Indeed, the bisons on the walls were drawn with multiple sets of legs, as if to suggest motion.

Walt Disney cites these paintings in his *History of Animation* as the precursor to the animated film.

In the caves' security the hunters could allow their emotions to simulate those experienced in the actual hunt. In complete safety they could wallow in fear. Later, in the hunt, recalling the cave experience they could successfully steel themselves against surrendering to their panic, which, thanks to the caves, was now familiar to them.

Stampeding bisons today pose no great danger to modern men and women. What authentic peril confronts us? In an everyday sense, the greatest immediate hazard has to be the automobile. Since 1945 alone nearly ten times as many

Americans have died in car crashes as in all the collected theaters of World War II.

Is it any wonder movies are replete with car crashes?

What else besides auto wrecks represents a genuine daily threat to our lives and our serenity? Crime. Disease. War. Broken families. Broken hearts. And are these not perpetually the stuff of films? Clearly, the movie theater is the modern-day version of the primitives' cave. A film is a life simulator enabling modern men and women to rehearse their emotions, to experience desperate, painful sensations in an environment of total safety.

Movies, therefore, offer a lot more than mere fun, though the best of them provide that, too. Like the cave people, our very survival depends upon our ability to deal with intensely painful emotions. If movie art permits us to accomplish this, then film is as fundamental to our spirits and souls as food to our flesh and bone. Cultures deprived of artistic expression warp and distort as surely as famine bends children's spines.

The hard fact is that our daily lives are racked not so much with pain as with tedium. Our hours overflow with trivial chores of endless, petty dimension. Sadly, the predominant feeling experienced by most people most of the time is no feeling at all but rather the absence of feeling— numbness, boredom. If art is first and foremost concerned with feeling, then it should come as no surprise that artists are people who experience feelings intensely. When they feel bad they feel despondent, even suicidal. When they feel good they feel ecstatic.

Screenwriters should embrace screenwriting for what it truly is: the business of feeling.

Ego

As asserted in the introduction to this book, writers hate to write; the prospect each day of addressing blank pages or glowing computer screens fills every one of them with dread. People who work alone, cooped up by themselves in their own little closet day after day, filing their feelings, trafficking in emotions, toiling literally to hock their dreams, easily develop into obstinate, prickly characters. For professional fantasizing is not without its hazards. And foremost among these is the ever-diminishing capacity to discriminate the real from the reel.

At a recent dinner party, while I was recounting some breathtakingly clever anecdote, my wife, privy to the actual events, interrupted, exclaiming, "But that's not how it really was."

Instead of overturning the table in a blind rage precipitated by her wrecking my punch line, in patient, measured tones I rejoined that selected embellishments help tell a tale better.

"There's a difference between selected embellishments," she said, "and pure fantasy."

"Pure fantasy," I insisted, "is what I do for a living. It's my work."

"But you're not at work now," she said. "You're at dinner with friends."

Simmering in superior intellectual juices, I silently contemplated what nonwriters can never understand: For a writer, dinner with friends is work; lying in the sun is work; visiting the powder room is work; sleeping and dreaming is work.

Is it any wonder that people who embrace such grandiose notions about themselves and their calling are likely to be awkward when it comes to social skills?

This difficulty daily confronts not screenwriters alone but all working writers. For screenwriters, however, the problem is exponentially more troublesome. Novelists and poets, for example, enjoy total control over their writing. Their work is their work; nobody comes between artist and art, nobody "improves" it, nobody is brought in to "punch it up" or "tone it down." To them accrues all credit and blame. To a somewhat more limited extent this is true also for playwrights, who are present week after week during rehearsals, and who are consulted on every script change. Indeed, not a word in a play can be changed without the playwright's consent.

This is a far cry from the experience of screenwriters, who, on those rare occasions when one of their scripts actually films, are likely to be banished from the set. And they are rewritten mercilessly, perhaps dozens of times, even when their scripts are not filmed, until the work is often no longer recognizable.

So screenwriters have more than ample occasion to suffer; such working conditions do not attract well-balanced, integrated, fulfilled personalities.

Not long ago a friend of mine was introduced to Julius J. Epstein, whose screenwriting credits include, among many others, *Casablanca.*

"Oh, Mr. Epstein," my friend gushed in breathy awe, "I am positively thrilled to meet you. All I or any of my up-and-coming film-phony friends ever hope is that just once in our lives we might become associated as you have with something bigger than ourselves, something timeless, something celebrated into eternity like *Casablanca.*"

Did Epstein say "Thank you very much," or "How kind of you to say so"?

He did not.

Instead he said, "Yeah? *Casablanca?* Well, I'll tell you something about *Casablanca,* since you brought it up. You know the part in the end where Claude Rains tells Bogart the thing about a beautiful friendship and all that? Originally it was supposed to be something else, a line was added which made the whole thing much more effective, something I had worked out at great length, in considerable detail, but no, Bogart had his own ideas—isn't that an actor for you?—and Curtiz, the director, he had some notion about some other thing—isn't that a director for you?—and even my own agents, betraying their loyalty to me, conspired with the rest of them against me and I tell you the picture would have been so much better if they had left it as I had it."

That's a working writer for you. Not only incapable of fielding a simple compliment, he sees in it instead an occasion for still further griping. Griping about what? About how the producers and agents and actors and directors ruined his work some forty years ago. And precisely what work did they ruin? *Casablanca!*

Please, God, let somebody ruin *my* work!

William Goldman is another example of a rich, respected writer with vast acclaim in novels, nonfiction, and film (*Butch Cassidy and the Sundance Kid, All the President's Men, Marathon Man, The Princess Bride,* and many others) who in print manages shamelessly to carp and complain about how miserably he has been mistreated on project after project.

Goldman's invaluable book, *Adventures in the Screen Trade,* eloquently articulates his experiences writing films. No screenwriter—veteran or rookie—should fail to own a copy. Still, for all its insights and contributions it is also replete with abuses and indignities heaped unceremoniously upon the beleaguered author by folks famous and obscure. Dustin Hoffman was rude when they worked together on a couple of pictures. Worse still, Robert Redford wouldn't even give Goldman his home phone number.

He couldn't just call Redford directly, no; he had to go through Redford's secretary!

I have a friend who is a successful studio musician whose career consists largely of playing background tracks for top recording artists. Not too many years ago he had his own solo record. A copy of the album arrived at my house at precisely the same moment as a mutual pal. He spotted the album.

"He makes records?"

"But you know he's made hundreds of recordings," I replied.

"Yeah," the pal said, "but solo? He makes money on that record?"

"Money?" The record in question was in fact highly experimental, not at all geared for the mass market. "I doubt it shipped platinum," I said, borrowing record trade jargon for a colossal best-seller. "Maybe it breaks even, or perhaps he even realizes some modest honorarium."

"In other words," the friend said, "it's just an ego trip."

I was taken aback; there seemed something so pejorative in the pronouncement. And then, in a flash I heard myself saying, "Yes! That's exactly what it is! An ego trip!"

For the first time in my life it occurred to me how deeply integrated into art is ego. There is, of course, much more to art than ego alone, but there's no escaping the fact that creative expression entails—indeed requires—no small involvement with ego.

Consider, for example, the ego necessary to a violinist.

A violin is, after all, not much more than an elegantly carved wooden box strung with cat's intestines across which is drawn horsehair in order to produce a sound. If you own a rare, innate talent, and if you devote every day of your life to constant, daily discipline, you can learn to wield hair and gut in such a fashion as to produce a sound that is somehow beautiful, ideally a sound people will even pay for the privilege of hearing.

There are a handful of folks who have made a considerable living doing precisely that. Imagine the ego required for such a scam!

And imagine the ego of, say, a Vincent van Gogh expecting people to support him in exchange for his applying colored pigment to blank canvas in what appears, at least on the surface, to be a fairly haphazard manner. A photograph of a sunflower, for example, is certainly a more accurate depiction than any mere painting by Vincent.

Some years ago, during contract negotiations, an actor friend participated in Screen Actors Guild meetings over the question of billing. Billing refers specifically to the manner in which on-screen credits are displayed, their relative size, time, whether a name stands on the screen by itself or is combined with others.

After hours of wrangling, weighing, arguing, a member stood up abruptly and barked, "Billing! Ridiculous! Whose name goes where? Above the title or below the title? What size typeface? Absurd! This is nothing but ego! That's all it is: ego!"

The group sat there quietly, righteously chastised, until another member slowly arose from his chair.

"Bet your damn life it's ego," he said. "Why in the world should we have to apologize for it?" He scanned the room. "Those are our faces up there, our flesh and blood. Those noises are our own and only voices. Why in the world ought we not accommodate our egos?"

In fact, for screenwriters and actors alike, screen credit involves much more than ego alone.

It involves money.

First, an artist's billing reflects his professional stature within the film and television industry. For the most part, if audiences care about actors they could not care less about who wrote or directed a film, any more than they care who was the chief electrician, who was the key grip. These have significance exclusively within the professional community. But a film artist's fee is closely linked to his billing. As billing status rises and falls, so also does remuneration.

Still more directly, billing is contractually connected to writers' financial compensation. Even so small a consideration as the word *and* instead of an ampersand (&) between two names can result in differences of literally millions of dollars. Two writers connected by an ampersand, for example, are considered a team, a single unit, each receiving only half as much profit share as a name separated from the others by the word *and*.

The purpose here is not to nail down all nuances pertinent to billing. I hope simply to state quite directly that screenwriters should allow themselves to flex their egos. Anyone who writes for the screen, who expects his fantasies to be worth sharing, who expects audiences to trade cash for the privilege of that sharing, had better be abundantly supplied with ego and self-esteem.

Criticism

Some years ago I collaborated with another writer on a comedy for a New York producer. Holed up in a borrowed apartment on the Upper West Side, we worked like slaves until at last we had a solid draft.

We took the one and only copy of the script, the typed original, to a shop to be photocopied, but stopped off along the way to grab a bite.

After gorging on hot and spicy squid, we returned to the car only to discover it had been burglarized; the attaché case containing the script was gone.

"Let's not panic," I said calmly, at which point we promptly panicked. Searching blindly in every direction we overturned garbage cans, upended litter baskets, frantically combed the gutters in every direction in the hope that the culprit had abandoned the case's contents nearby.

Sure enough, away down at the end of a dark alley we spotted what appeared in the shadows to be a tossed-away attaché case with scattered pages flowing from its broken lid. While I waited at the curb holding my breath, my partner walked the alley's length and emerged moments later, thumbing through our script.

"What do you know about that?" he said, peering closely at the pages. "The guy made comments on it." Squinting at phantom letters, he pretended to read aloud: "Dialogue stilted, theme meretricious."

My collaborator was, of course, kidding. But in fact when it comes to movies, everybody's a critic.

It is a burden screenwriters must bear. And more than merely bear it, they must learn how to welcome criticism, how to seek and solicit it. Finally, and most important, they must learn how to turn criticism around, to transform what might at first appear negative and destructive into something useful. Criticism is part of screenwriting's routine; writers must remain available to it, must exploit it, must use it to help sculpt and reshape their scripts.

In truth, all any writer wants to hear upon completing a draft is that it is perfect, brilliant, life-changing, eternal. Anything less engenders despair, a slashing of confidence and wrists.

To reiterate, screenwriting's purpose is first and foremost to provoke intense, passionate feelings. And again, people drawn to such an endeavor inevitably experience their emotions strongly. If civilians are easily hurt when criticized, for writers the experience is excruciating.

Inexperienced writers typically figure, incorrectly, that once they achieve some skill, once they win success, criticism ends. Who dares criticize an established, respected writer?

The answer is, everybody. The more successful a writer becomes, the more widely distributed is his work and the greater the target he presents to critics.

Worse still, the greater a writer's success, the greater the jealousy engendered among both the public and his colleagues (and competitors) within the arts community.

What is important for writers to learn about handling criticism is not merely to be polite even when it is unsolicited, or unsound, or downright stupid, but somehow to remain open to that odd, slim fragment that might prove useful.

To get the kinks out of my joints after a day's slaving at the word processor, I swim. Recently, toweling off in the locker room I was approached by a young fellow who addressed me in a harsh tone and with a curious effect. "Enjoy your swim?" he said with something like anger.

"Yes, thanks," I muttered. As he continued to stare, I heard myself asking, "You?"

"Me?" he responded. "How can I swim? I'm the lifeguard. I have to sit there watching you. And you know what? I don't like what I see."

Instead of calling Campus Security, I inquired, "What do you mean?"

"First, you're chopping your stroke, cutting it short, squandering its full thrust. Second, your head rides too low in the water. Third, . . ." Unsolicited, he continued to catalogue all the atrocities I commit when moist. Notwithstanding his lack of social graces, there appeared a faint but certain authority in his pronouncements.

The next day I tried out his suggestions in the pool.

I will not say that it felt good; quite the contrary, changing my style made me feel awkward. Nevertheless, when I was through, the clock revealed to me that I had substantially cut my time; clearly my swimming had improved, further evidence of the fact that all people—swimmers, writers—need stay open to criticism, no matter how unwelcome, no matter how useless it may at first appear.

Some years ago an agent offered what struck me at the time as a uniquely worthless suggestion regarding a draft of a script I had just written. Instead of telling him that it was the dumbest notion I'd ever heard, I stated in a perfectly civil tone that his was a thought I'd certainly explore, all the while thinking how presumptuous he, a mere agent, had been to offer any suggestion at all. I'm the writer, I said to myself in silence, you're the salesman: Sell!

And for weeks I stewed quietly in the venom generated by this broker's presumption. Then, months later, rewriting the script, I suddenly came up with what I took to be a brilliant and original notion, something that solved a host of story problems. After basking in self-satisfaction, I was abruptly humbled when all at once it occurred to me that I had merely incorporated the agent's suggestion. I did this not as a concession to him, but purely in service to improved writing.

Writers do not, therefore, need to respect critics; they need merely respect criticism. And respecting does not mean accepting. Remaining open to criticism is not the same thing as indiscriminately agreeing.

Dumb, negative, jealous, destructive, backbiting criticism is by no means the only problem writers face. Affirmation can be a problem too. For if approval is a lot more fun than scorn, it can be every bit as deadly. It is a short walk, after all, from praise to patronization. And all artists are suckers for praise.

When my first novel was published, an undermining, crazy-making colleague at the university constantly asked me for a copy. Clearly, he was not willing actually to purchase the book. Insincerely I promised eventually to lend it to him, but forever put him off. Finally, catching me unawares at my office one day, he spotted a copy of the book, seized it, and fled.

I figured that was just one less copy of the book to offer some deserving soul. The next day he was back in my office returning the book, which, as it turned out, he had actually read. Lustily he sang its praises, complimenting "the broad, rich story, the flesh-and-blood characters, the sweet, punchy, yet poetic dialogue." Somehow I found myself figuring I had underestimated this fellow. He wasn't such a bad guy after all. Had I not misjudged his perception, his taste? In two seconds flat I was his slave simply because he liked my book, and I'm his grateful slave to this day!

Rejection and Heartache

Finishing a script tends to bring screenwriters far more despair than joy.

There are essentially two reasons for this. First, day by day, hard at work upon a screenplay, a writer knows just what to do with himself: Write the script. To complete the draft is to be cast adrift. Often there sets in a quiet panic. Happily, that eventually gives way. Sadly, what it gives way to is a deep, dark depression.

As already discussed in Chapter 3, it is far harder to finish a script than to begin, because until the script is complete there is no possibility of having it criticized and rejected. And even the finest scripts engender their fair share of negative comment. No one has to wait in line for his ration of nit-picking.

There are two remedies.

First and foremost, after taking the shortest breather, a writer should move right on to his next project. Writing is always the writer's best defense. Instead of sitting by the phone, eating out his heart with a spoon, forever awaiting an agent's or producer's reaction, a writer should be hard at work writing. It sure beats corroding the stomach lining in anticipation of the right or the wrong phone call.

Finally, writers have to learn how to allow themselves to feel lousy for a while.

To the writer's substantial advantage, he may endure scores of rejections, but he requires only a single acceptance. Tales abound of movies rejected everywhere, year after year, finally to be sold, filmed, and turned into critical, financial successes. Oliver Stone's *Platoon* is a fair example. Stone, already a power to be reckoned with, owning a track record including such successes as *Midnight Express,* peddled *Platoon* around Hollywood for a decade before getting it to the screen.

No writer, therefore, no matter how respected, no matter how successful, is above rejection. Instead of being "intelligent" about it, instead of being rational and enlightened, the writer needs to gnaw on his heart and his soul for perhaps a couple of days.

Upon encountering rejection, writers should not waste time and energy defending their work. A script is its own best argument for itself. And when scripts are rejected, instead of engaging the rejector in a shrill exchange about how right the writer and wrong the reader, instead of discussing potential rewrites and revisions, writers should learn simply to recite: "Thank you for your attention and consideration."

And then they should take their script elsewhere.

Years ago I wrote a script speculatively, only to have it rejected by the first agent to whom it was offered. When I inquired—foolishly—what precisely it was that he had found lacking, he said that he had found its story thin, its characters shallow, its dialogue amateurish, its scenes and settings unimaginative, its theme devoid of merit, its incidents and anecdotes familiar and pedestrian.

With a perfectly straight face, I told him that he needn't spare my feelings, that if he didn't like the script he should say so; I assured him I could take it.

The humorless broker responded: "But I *am* saying so!"

I am able to relate this experience with no small joy because I went directly across the street (Sunset Boulevard) and delivered the script to another agent who read it and eagerly agreed to represent it. He secured a cash offer two weeks later.

Possibly, after a slew of rejections, and especially if the criticism seems to be generally consistent, a writer may want to hold onto a script for a while and restudy it, possibly with an eye toward reworking. Or he may decide simply to abandon a script.

Every experienced writer has scripts he has written—among them ones that have sold, in some cases scripts that have even been filmed—that now, given his growth, he would never show. Writers need to learn how to let go of a script, how to lose their focus on the past and affix their vision instead to the present and the future. If a writer is successful, sometimes after he has let go of a script it may very well come to be rewritten by one or several other writers.

In Chapter 8 the necessity for rewriting is discussed at length. The process can be arduous in the extreme. But being rewritten by others can be still more painful. Nevertheless, it is part of screenwriting's nature, and writers need to learn how to accept it.

Many producers throw another writer, or team of writers, upon a script simply because they do not know what else to do. They may consider the original writer "written out," or they may see hiring and firing writers as their only function after assigning parking places.

The plain truth is, pain aside, it is a privilege for a writer to be rewritten. When a studio hires writers to rewrite your work, while you may view it as testimony to their dissatisfaction with your effort, in fact it may mean just the opposite. Personally, I reject the notion—dear to the heart of too many producers—that with screenwriting two heads, or three, or four or five, are better than one. That may be true for designing toasters, tires, or tea bags, but screenwriting is subjective. Objectivity is for other endeavors, not art.

Nevertheless, when a studio regards a project as hopeless, it cuts its losses and drops the script. When it hires additional writers, thereby committing additional money, this is evidence of faith

There is at UCLA an instructor of ceramics whose beginning students, upon completing their first project, are required to smash it against the wall.

This is simply to instill in the students a healthy respect for the distance required between artists and their art. For the true artist's art, like his child, is of him, from him, like him. It resembles him in so many ways, but it is not he. He is he and it is it. The notion may appear obvious, but for artists it is a difficult, critical distinction to embrace.

And if it is difficult for writers, consider actors. Writers certainly suffer when their scripts are rejected, but their scripts are still just that: their scripts. When an actor is rejected it is his voice, his look, his posture, his walk, his smell, his flesh, his blood that are adjudged to be wanting.

And so when writers sink into deep despair as is from time inevitable, they ought to consider actors. I often think the reason there are actors is simply so that there should be one group treated more rudely, suffering more profoundly than writers.

Good art hurts. That is one important part of its nature. That is testimony to its integral role in our lives. Creative expression, as Bronowski asserts, is uniquely human. It derives from our facility to visualize the future, to anticipate it, to represent it in images we project in our head, or on the wall of a cave, or upon a movie screen.

Recommended Reading

With new screenwriting books appearing these days at a breathless clip, there is still not one that touches Aristotle's *Poetics* for insights into story structure. There is, of course, no small irony in the fact that this screenwriter's bible—really not much more than a pamphlet—was written over two millennia before film was even invented.

Screenwriters are not expected ever fully to understand the *Poetics*. Rather, they have to study it again and again. They have to make it part of their lives. It need not be read straight through from beginning to end; one can skip around at random. The trick to using the *Poetics* is not to try to extract timeless principles, though they are surely there, but rather to follow it closely in a practical, hands-on way, not to interpret but obey.

My beloved and esteemed colleague at UCLA, writer/producer/educator Lew Hunter, alerted me years ago to another book not intended for screenwriters at all yet one with much to offer us. Dorothea Brande's *Becoming a Writer* (New York: Harcourt, Brace, 1934) is fifty years ahead of its time in addressing right brain/left brain considerations, the integration of reasoned, methodical analysis on one hand with spontaneous creativity on the other.

Brande pays much attention to day-to-day working methods, going so far as to advise writers precisely what to read—and even what *not* to read—while at work on a project. She gives us permission to skim silly, superficial fare—tabloids, comics, matchbooks, cereal boxes. Even better, she urges us to avoid weighty, philosophical tomes. What is more, she recommends practical techniques to help writers free themselves should they become stuck.

And what writer doesn't from time to time become stuck?

Writer/critic Walter Kerr wrote a delightful and enormously enlightening slim volume aimed at playwrights: *How Not to Write a Play* (London: Max Reinhardt, 1956). It is a splendidly accessible work, stern but affectionate, and frequently quite funny. It humbles writers who become caught up in self-importance. And it reminds us that if art is choice, choosing what to include is not a bit more important than choosing what to leave out.

Another unlikely book of substantial value for screenwriters is *The Fifty Worst Films of All Time* by Harry Medved and Randy Dreyfuss (New York: Popular Library, 1978). Far from the rip-and-slash cynicism the title might fairly be expected to portend, here instead is a reasoned, responsible, affirmative analysis of what goes wrong with so many well-intentioned films, both famous and obscure.

The Fifty Worst Films of All Time is replete with histories as well as reviews. The sections on *Last Year at Marienbad* and *Ivan the Terrible, Parts One* and *Two* are especially worthy. Quoting from the book's treatment of the latter: "The average filmgoer should trust his own instincts in reacting to film. The fact that a movie is overwrought and boring does not mean that it is somehow edifying or 'good for you.' " Here is valuable advice not merely for filmgoers—the authors' intended readership—but for film writers as well.

When the authors wrote *The Fifty Worst Films of All Time,* the senior among them, Dreyfuss, was not yet twenty.

Medved, two years younger, was a high school kid. Yet theirs is an accomplishment of authentic maturity.

William Goldman's *Adventures in the Screen Trade* (New York: Warner Books, 1983) is a painful, wry, fascinating book containing slings, arrows, nuts, bolts, and a vast compendium of information screenwriters, established or aspiring, will find useful. The most recent edition, widely available as a trade paperback, contains Goldman's complete screenplay for *Butch Cassidy and the Sundance Kid* in its original typed format. A writer of Goldman's stature gets away with various quirks of style that the rest of us might well avoid. It would be a mistake, therefore, to use his *Butch . . .* as a model for all screenplay format. Still, it is certainly worthwhile for anyone interested in seeing what one particularly respected script really looks like, straight from the writer's desk.

Another book that avoids the mistake of printing screenplays in a sanitized format is *Five Screenplays by Preston Sturges* (Berkeley: University of California Press, 1985), edited by Brian Henderson. Sturges was, of course, one of Hollywood's original geniuses. His timeless scripts are presented here photocopied from the original typed pages. In addition to the scripts themselves are photographs and histories plus all sorts of information pertinent to the daily slugging-it-out routine belonging to all writers fortunate enough to be permitted to suffer so thoroughly and so long in Hollywood.

Another book from the same publisher is *Backstory—Interviews With Screenwriters of Hollywood's Golden Age* (1986), edited by Pat McGilligan. Like Goldman's *Adventures in the Screen Trade,* it provides a firsthand look at the daily struggle all too familiar to some of film's most respected artists. It's the good and bad news for writers who succeed.

*   *   *

Another such work, too long out of print, is William Froug's *The Screenwriter Looks at the Screenwriter* (New York: Macmillan, 1972). The screenwriting community would be well served by a new edition of this pioneering excursion into working screenwriters' hearts and souls. Their agonies, ecstasies, frustrations, and rewards are more informative than scores of books treating theory.

A similar volume, although it deals not with screenwriters but playwrights, is Toby Cole's *Playwrights on Playwriting* (New York: Hill and Wang, 1960). As already asserted, playwrights and movie writers share the same basic problem: how to be worthy of an audience. Cole has comments from Ibsen and Chekhov through O'Neill to Ionesco and Osborne. The section on Arthur Miller is particularly useful, especially regarding the ways in which all dramatists, regardless of format, need to learn to let go of preconceived notions of character and theme and to find these quantities during the act of writing.

Bruno Bettelheim's modern classic, *The Uses of Enchantment* (New York: Knopf, 1977), offers breakthrough insights into the nature of human imagination and fantasy, the essence of story and dream. There is much here meriting screenwriters' attention.

After more than twenty years I recently reread Marshall McLuhan's *Understanding Media: The Extensions of Man,* (New York: McGraw-Hill, 1964), fully expecting it to appear weary and frail, just so much groovy sixties pop-babble. Instead, it shines more brightly than ever. McLuhan was anything but a shuck-and-jive artist; more clearly than anybody he saw the Big Picture. Like no other seer he appreciates the way things break apart and, far more importantly for artists, the way they come together. For any screenwriter who wants to do likewise, *Understanding Media* is a must-read and must-read-again.

* * *

Additional Dialogue (New York: Bantam, 1972), edited by Helen Manfull, consists of superstar screenwriter Dalton Trumbo's collected letters over his first twenty years in Hollywood, starting during early World War II, through the blacklisting era, and into the early sixties. The book's main focus is the politics of the age, and the special suffering of writers unable to write under their own names or, worse, unable to write at all. Through it all there is much commentary, which transcends the immediate situation and applies to essential screenwriting problems.

My own mentor from the University of Southern California's golden age in the late 1960s, Irwin R. Blacker, has had published posthumously *The Elements of Screenwriting—A Guide for Film and Television Writers* (New York: Macmillan, 1986), a manual modeled after Strunk and White's classic *Elements of Style.* Blacker, an eccentric but affectionate soul, was a serious scholar and novelist in addition to having had substantial experience in film and television. His *Elements . . .* is the final among dozens of books he made time to write during a busy career teaching, story-editing, and writing.

At USC he influenced all of the legendary students, including Lucas, Milius, Kleiser, Richter, Huyck, Barwood, Robbins, and legions of others. It is no exaggeration to suggest that through these film artists his influence now reaches billions of people around the globe and continues to grow. In the late-sixties swamp of let-it-all-hang-out and do-your-own-thing, Blacker was a lone warrior for discipline and structure, for story, for strong characterization, for vigorous, abrupt, to-the-point dialogue.

Two books worthy of attention are Dr. Linda Seger's *How to Make a Good Script Great* (New York: Dodd, Mead, 1987) and Viki King's *Inner Movie Method* (New York: Harper and Row, 1987). Dr. Seger is a script consultant widely respected in the professional film community. Her book deals primarily with that dreadful but necessary challenge facing all writers: the rewrite. The volume is liberally laced with examples from scripts. Viki King's book has a wondrously offbeat creative slant and contains methods of visualization geared toward freeing writers' imaginations.

In the present volume I refer now and again to Jacob Bronowski's television series, *The Ascent of Man*. The series is reprised in print (Boston: Little, Brown, 1973), and belongs in every writer's library. It is but one among many books Bronowski wrote during his lifetime. Another worthy of screenwriters' attention is *The Face of Violence*.

Television writer/producer Bob Shanks has written two books treating the small screen. The first, *The Cool Fire*, is more philosophical than the second, *The Primarly Screen*, which deals with writing films especially intended for television. *Primal Screen* (New York: Fawcett, 1986) contains Shanks's entire teleplay for *Drop-Out Father* and offers writers a firsthand look at TV movie script format. Both books are of value to screenwriters.

In this book I refer to what was for me a lifelong blind spot: physics and mathematics. Some years ago, working on a screenplay requiring research into those areas, I was enabled to appreciate the close connection between the working methodologies belonging to artists and scientists. Three first-rate books easily accessible to lay readers are *Taking the Quantum Leap* by Fred Alan Wolf (New York: Harper and Row, 1981), *Einstein for Beginners* by Joseph Schwartz and Michael McGuinness (New York: Pantheon, 1979), and, most especially, Lincoln Barnett's *The Universe and Doctor Einstein* (New York: Harper and Brothers, 1948). These books may not seem to be worth a great deal to screenwriters, but, in fact, each has far more to offer than any ten volumes on screenplay format or script marketing.

*   *   *

All people who hope to work in the public and popular arts will serve themselves wisely by reading Steven Bach's best-selling *Final Cut* (New York: Morrow, 1985). While most of the attention it receives revolves around the Hollywood gossip pertaining to Michael Cimino's antics in the unmaking of *Heaven's Gate,* its greatest value lies in the early chapters treating the history of United Artists and, particularly, the false dichotomy separating art on the one hand from commerce on the other. Bach eloquently consigns to its rightful resting place the widespread erroneous notion that in mass art there is an inevitably adversarial relationship between artistic quality and market success.

Finally, every writer who is smart enough to care about how he is perceived by others needs to have constantly at his side not one but several dictionaries. I keep a small one for quick checking of spelling and a large, unabridged volume for deeper considerations of language questions. Beyond these, of course, I refer now and again to one of the world's great history books: the two-volume micro-print edition of the *Oxford English Dictionary*. Additionally, I always have on hand my Roget's *Thesaurus* and a collection of grammar and punctuation guides. My favorite is *The Perrin Writer's Guide and Index to English* (Scott, Foresman and Company, 1942), which is now out of print. See also *The Mentor Guide to Punctuation* (New American Library, 1986) and *The New American Dictionary of Good English* (New American Library, 1987).